FUTURE EDGE

FUTURE EDGE

Discovering the New Paradigms
of Success

Joel Arthur Barker

WILLIAM MORROW AND COMPANY, INC.
NEW YORK

It is the policy of William Morrow and Company, Inc., and its imprints and affiliates, recognizing the importance of preserving what has been written, to print the books we publish on acid-free paper, and we exert our best efforts to that end.

Library of Congress Cataloging-in-Publication Data

Barker, Joel Arthur.
    Future edge : discovering the new paradigms of success / by
Joel Arthur Barker.
       p.   cm.
    ISBN 0-688-10936-5
    1. Business forecasting. 2. Forecasting. 3. Paradigms (Social
sciences) 4. Success in business. I. Title.
HD30.27.B36   1992
658.4'0355—dc20   91-27583
                                             CIP

Printed in the United States of America

First Edition

1 2 3 4 5 6 7 8 9 10

BOOK DESIGN BY LYNN DOROFINO DESIGNS

To my mother and father who were never bothered by my being a little weird;

To my wife and partner, Susan, who has never
wavered in her support;

And to my son, Andrew, who was and still is my
greatest teacher

Acknowledgments

WHILE THE WRITING of a book is a solitary activity, the experiences and help that prepared me came from many people over the past two decades. I would like to thank, in particular, those people who helped me at the crucial times in my development as a futurist and author.

Thanks to **Tom Read** for giving me permission to leave my teaching position at St. Paul Academy and Summit School to explore what the futures studies movement was all about; to **David Lilly** for providing the funds for that fellowship; to **Dennis Meadows,** childhood friend, who gave me a chance to study the questions of Limits to Growth with his team in Copenhagen; to Professor **James Bright,** who became my first mentor in the field of futures studies; to **T. Lance Holthusen,** who brought me into the Science Museum of Minnesota and then promoted me into his own job as director of the Futures Studies Department because he thought I could do a better job; to my wife, **Susan,** for encouraging me to take the leap and become an independent consultant and lecturer; to **Bill Weimer,** mentor and friend, who was first to recognize the deep importance of the paradigm discussion for corporations and gave me my first contact with IBM; to **Scott Erickson,** my friend and partner, who always challenged me to improve my work on paradigms; to **Ray Christensen,** who had the courage to partner with me in the making of my video *Discovering the Future: The Business of Paradigms;* to **Jaymie Mitchell,** who helped me with the graphic preparation of my manuscript; to **Margret McBride,** my wonderful agent, who brought me to William Morrow and my most excellent editor, **Adrian Zackheim.**

Contents

Foreword

FOR THE PAST FOUR YEARS I have been describing three keys to the future for any organization, profit or nonprofit, that wants to participate fully in the twenty-first century.

They are:

Anticipation

Innovation

Excellence

When I ask my audiences if they agree with the importance of three "keys," they always do. It is hard to argue with them. And yet many organizations think one or two of the three are enough.

All three are necessary.

Let me tell you why.

11

Excellence is at the base of the list because it is the base of the twenty-first century. Many in my audiences justify the importance of excellence (or Total Quality Management, as it is also called) because they believe it will give them a competitive edge in the twenty-first century. I don't believe that. I say it will give them a competitive edge only until the end of the decade. After that, it becomes the necessary price of entry.

If you do not have the components of excellence—statistic process control, continuous improvement, benchmarking, the constant pursuit of excellence, the capability of knowing how to do the right thing the first time (all of these derive from the same philosophy created by W. Edwards Deming and O. M. Juran and universalized by them and people like Philip Crosby)—then **you don't even get to play the game.**

Innovation is on the list because it **is** the way you gain competitive edge. Innovation coupled with excellence—which the Japanese have done so well—is a powerful combination. In the twenty-first century, no one will always be the leader. The top four or five positions within an industry will change frequently. But it is in the top four or five positions that you want to be. Lower than that will require you to price your copycat products at a commodity level, and that will leave you with insufficient margin to pay for the research and development necessary to work your way up to the top level.

However, excellence and innovation are not enough.

Anticipation provides you with the information that allows you to be in the right place at the right time with your excellent innovative product or service.

Too many times we have seen great ideas arrive too late: the Univac personal computer, Federal Express Zap mail. And we have also seen great ideas arrive too early: AT&T Picturephone; Apple's Macintosh (lucky for Steve Jobs that Steve Wozniak stuck to the knitting with the Apple II, which allowed the Macintosh to wait for its right time—desktop publishing time).

Anticipation is the final element of the triad. This triad allows you to predict your customer needs, innovate the products or services required to fulfill them, and produce those products and services excellently. With these three attributes you are ready not just to survive in the twenty-first century but to thrive!

This book is about innovation and anticipation. It will make you better at both.

The future is where our greatest leverage is.

CHAPTER 1

Watching for the Future

LET ME share with you a true story that began in 1968. It illustrates why we need to learn how to explore the future.

In 1968, if anyone had been asked the following question, you would have expected the same answer: In 1990 what nation will dominate the world of watchmaking?

The answer—Switzerland.

Why? Because Switzerland had dominated the world of watchmaking for the past sixty years. The Swiss made the best watches in the world. Anyone who wanted a good watch, an accurate watch, bought a Swiss watch.

And the Swiss were constantly improving their watches. They had invented the minute hand and the second hand. They led the research in discovering better ways to manufacture the gears, the bearings, and the mainsprings of modern watches. They were on the cutting edge of research in waterproofing watches. They brought to market the best self-winding watches. They were constant innovators.

What I am trying to point out is that the Swiss didn't just rest on their laurels. They continually worked at making better watches.

By 1968 they had done so well that they had more than 65 percent of the unit sales in the world watch market and more than 80 percent of the profits (some experts estimated as high as 90 percent). They were the world leaders in watchmaking by an enormous stretch. No one was even a close second.

Yet by 1980 their market share had collapsed from 65 percent to less than 10 percent. Their huge profit domination had dropped to less than 20 percent. By all significant measures, they had been ignominiously dethroned as the world market leader.

What happened?

Something profound.

They had run into a **paradigm shift**—a change in the fundamental rules of watchmaking. The mechanical mechanism was about to give way to electronics. Everything the Swiss were good at—the making of gears and bearings and mainsprings—was irrelevant to the new way.

And so, in less than ten years, the Swiss watchmaking future, which had seemed so secure, so profitable, so dominant, was destroyed. Between 1979 and 1981, fifty thousand of the sixty-two thousand watchmakers lost their jobs. And, in a nation as small as Switzerland, it was a catastrophe.

For another nation, however, it was the opportunity of a lifetime. Japan, which had less than 1 percent of the world watch market in 1968 (even though their mechanical watches were almost as good as those of the Swiss), was in the midst of developing world-class electronic technology. The electronic quartz watch was a natural derivative. Seiko led the charge, and today the Japanese have about 33 percent of the market, with an equivalent share of the profits.

The irony of this story for the Swiss is that the situation was totally avoidable if only the Swiss watch manufacturers had known how to think about their own future. If only they had known the kind of change they were facing: a paradigm shift.

Because it was the Swiss themselves who invented the electronic quartz movement at their research institute in Neuchâtel, Switzerland. Yet, when the Swiss researchers presented this revolutionary new idea to the Swiss manufacturers in 1967, it was rejected.

After all, it didn't have a mainspring, it didn't need bearings, it required almost no gears, it was battery-powered, it was electronic. **It couldn't possibly be the watch of the future.** So sure were the manufacturers of that conclusion that they let their researchers showcase their useless invention at the World Watch Congress that year. Seiko took one look, and the rest is history.

How can you avoid the mistake the Swiss made? And, keep in mind, the Swiss watch industry isn't the only one that has made such a mistake. Nations have done it. Many corporations and organizations have done it. Individuals have done it. We are all susceptible.

My task is to help you avoid the Swiss mistake by improving your ability to anticipate the future.

Most people know the future only as a place that is always robbing them of their security, breaking promises, changing the rules on them, causing all sorts of troubles. And yet, **it is in the future where our greatest leverage is.** We can't change the past, although if we are smart, we learn from it. Things happen only in one place—the present. And usually we react to those events. The "space" of time in the present is too slim to allow for much more. It is in the yet-to-be, the future, and only there, where we have the time to prepare for the present.

If we can learn to anticipate the future better, we need not fear it. In fact, we can welcome it, embrace it, prepare for its coming, because more of it will be the direct outgrowth of our own efforts.

We may not be able to discern the exact size of the future, but we can surely do better, through exploration, in obtaining significant data about its probable outline and direction. In fact, we need to if we want to begin to shape our own future. We are going to focus on a single concept that can help us do a much better job of anticipating the future. And while we learn to anticipate, we will also learn how to be more innovative through both discovery and creation.

> **Why is that intelligent people with good motives do such a poor job at anticipating the future?**

We are going to examine several of the key principles that explain this apparent contradiction. These principles are embedded in a discussion of paradigms and how they change. These principles not only explain why people do not anticipate the future well; they explain how to improve your ability to see aspects of the future that may otherwise be totally invisible to you. And I promise you, because I have seen it repeatedly, that by understanding the Paradigm Principles you will be able to open doorways to your future that would have otherwise stayed locked up until it was too late. Just like the Swiss.

As more than one sage has already observed, the future is where you are going to spend the rest of your life. And since that is true, wouldn't it be useful to be able to get to know more about the neighborhood before you move in?

You can and should shape your own future. Because, if you don't, someone else surely will.

CHAPTER 2

The Importance of Anticipation

THE FIELD OF FUTURE STUDIES became familiar to the public when Alvin Toffler published his now classic *Future Shock* in 1970. That book demonstrated to a wide audience the importance of trying to anticipate the future, to understand potential long-term implications of change, both positive and negative, before they occurred.

Future studies, or futurism or futurology, already had a substantial although secluded life long before Toffler appeared on the scene. Study of the future began during World War II in the military and was continued after the war by the RAND Corporation, Stanford Research Institute (now SRI International), Ted Gordon's Futures Group, and the Hudson Institute. The concept of studying the future grew in a serious and rigorous way throughout the 1950s and 1960s.

But it took the social and political chaos and resulting turbulence of the 1970s to bring this field of study out of the scholarly closet and into the living room of public visibility. These days we expect to read articles about the future in popular magazines, to find books about the future in our local bookstore, and to watch TV shows whose primary purpose is to give us information about possible futures ahead. The study of the future is a part of our conceptual landscape because we, as members of a global society, have come to value the skills of anticipation.

The field of future studies can be broken up into two general areas: **content futurism** and **process futurism**. A content futurist is a person who specializes in an area of information about the future. Whether it is robotics or telecommunications, energy or water usage, shelter design or nutrition, content futurists speculate on the "whats" of the future. Process futurism, the area I have chosen to focus on, deals with **how** to think about the "whats." In my own work, I have often found that people have significant amounts of content about possible futures but have no way of making that information useful. Process futurists teach them how to manipulate that information.

I want to teach you about a concept that can help you to discover the future with greater accuracy. It is a way of fishing for the future.

In the last twenty years, all of Western society has passed through extraordinarily turbulent times. We have been living in a time when fundamental rules, the basic ways we do things, have been altered dramatically. That is, what was right and appropriate in the early 1960s is now, in many cases, wrong and highly inappropriate in the 1990s. Or, conversely, what was impossible, crazy, or clearly out of line in the early 1960s is, in many cases today, so ordinary that we forget that it wasn't always that way. These dramatic changes are extremely important because they have created in us a special sense of impermanence that generates tremendous discomfort.

Let's take a look at an abbreviated list of these fundamental changes in technology and society:

- The introduction of environmentalism (everything living is interconnected; there is no such thing as a free lunch) as a legitimate way of perceiving the world.

- Terrorism as an everyday activity.

- Rampant inflation in the United States during the 1970s and 1980s.

- Deregulation of banking, the airlines, the telecommunications and trucking industries.

- The loss of the United States's position as the leading-edge manufacturer of the world (for example, of VCRs).

- VCRs.

- Civil rights.

- The growth of participatory management in the United States.

- The loss of respect for major institutions such as the Supreme Court, the police, the federal government, the Congress.

- The almost total disappearance of union power.

- The emergence of information as a key resource.

- Public language on TV and radio incorporating cursing and strong sexual connotation within normal programming.

- Cohabitation as an acceptable substitute for marriage.

- The collapse of nuclear power as a viable energy option for the United States.

- A new appreciation of "small is beautiful" and the rejection of "big is always better."

- The common use of satellite communications.

- The disappearance of the idea that continual growth is automatically good.

- The vast amount of data exchanged via computers worldwide.

- The "uncloseting" of gays and other previously hidden minorities.

- Fiber optics.

- The new importance of the role of women in business and politics.

- Energy conservation as a new attitude in the United States.

- The women's movement.

- The growing necessity of cable TV.

- The number of people getting regular aerobic exercise every day.

- Breaking up of AT&T and the formation of the Baby Bells.

- Japan as a producer of the highest-quality products.

- Cellular phones.

- The collapse of the savings and loan industry.

- Faxing.

- Yogurt "ice cream."

- Rap music.

- Superconductivity at warmer temperatures.

- Safe sex.

- The Greenhouse Effect.

- The number of people eating a healthy diet by choice.

- The explosion of the use of personal computers in the home and at the office.

- Biotechnology.

- Republicans saying a large federal deficit is okay.

There are still many more examples I could cite, but the point is this: We have undergone extraordinary changes in the last thirty years in terms of the alteration of the old rules and regulations of our lives.

Now, let me ask a question: What if you had been able to anticipate some of those changes? What if you had known, for sure, about just one of those major changes? What would you have been able to do with that information?

For instance, what if you had anticipated the growth of personal computers? Let's say you did it in 1976 when it was still

only a gleam in two college dropouts' eyes. Think of the investment opportunities you could have had.

Or how about the move toward healthy, less fattening foods
like yogurt? Who would have guessed it would become so popular?

No matter who you are or what you do, it would have made
a big difference. At the very least you would have been subject
to less surprise, less "future shock." At the very most, you could
have made millions of dollars, perhaps even billions of dollars—if
you had had that knowledge. The leverage that is gained by
discovering these kinds of changes is profound, because these
rule changes are **not foreshadowed by trends.** That is why, for
many people, even (and, in some cases, especially) for the experts, they seem unpredictable.

> **These kinds of changes in the rules create new
> trends or dramatically alter trends already in
> place. That makes them very special.**

Here is a second question to consider: What innovations in
products and services were triggered by those changes? One only
need look at the change in attitudes about the environment to
understand the implications of this question. Whole new industries have sprung up around environmentalism. It will be a
trillion-dollar industry worldwide by the year 2000 and yet it
didn't exist in 1960.

The changes represented on the above list not only spawn
new trends, **they trigger cascades of innovations** that last for

decades. By knowing the nature of such changes and how to anticipate them, you can gain extraordinary leverage in shaping your own future.

Let's return to the word "anticipate" for a moment. Anticipation is the ability to foresee, to realize beforehand. Peter Drucker, in *Managing in Turbulent Times*, makes a very interesting observation. He writes about the skills that a good manager needs and suggests that one of the most important managerial skills during times of high turbulence is **anticipation**.

I strongly support Drucker's observation. Take a look at the graph (Figure 1). What you will find is that almost everyone who is successful in management has strong problem-solving skills, predominantly in the **reactive** mode. That is, when a real problem occurs, they solve it. While they spend most of their time problem solving, every so often they do move into the other quadrants. But the dominant way they run their lives is in the problem-solving/reaction mode.

There is, of course, good reason for this behavior. It is how they are judged for their effectiveness on the job. They are paid to solve problems, so it is natural they spend our time doing just that.

What Drucker is suggesting is that managers must improve their skills in the opposite quadrant of the grid: (A) that is, the area of anticipation and problem avoidance/opportunity identification. It is in this area that great leverage over the future can be generated—personally, corporately, nationally.

All of us, in fact, must move from the old style of solving real problems **after** they have occurred to the new style of an-

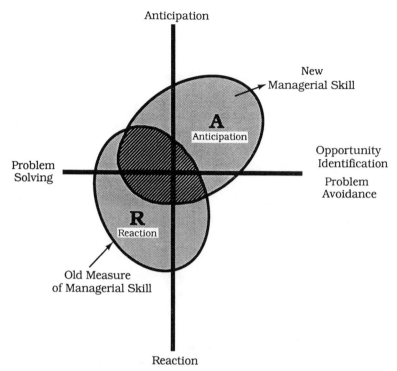

Figure 1—New Measure of Managerial Skill

ticipating potential problems before they happen and keeping them from occurring in the first place.

Here is a metaphor that illustrates Drucker's point in a different way. Think of a river: smooth, crystalline, sandy-bottomed, sandy-shored, slow, steady-flowing.

If someone said to you, "Look, I want you to get from this side of the river to the other side," it wouldn't be much of a challenge. All you would need to do is find a boat and a way to power the boat. The point is, to cross a river like that doesn't take much anticipation, because all the information you need is unambiguously in front of you.

Now, let's think about a different river, a highly turbulent one. It is filled with whirlpools and eddies and changes in the current. Because of its turbulence, it has churned up a lot of dirt from the bottom so that the water is opaque. It is filled with boulders that can't be seen. The shores on both sides have been eroded by the turbulence and are rocky and irregular.

If someone asks you to cross this river, it is fundamentally a different proposition. Here, in fact, anticipation will make a big difference in your success. If you can anticipate the rocks below the water, if you can anticipate the whirlpools and the changes in the current, if you can anticipate the landing on the other shore, you have a much better chance of getting across that river successfully.

The times we are living in are much like the turbulent river. And **in times of turbulence the ability to anticipate dramatically enhances your chances of success.**

But, to say that one should anticipate better doesn't explain how to anticipate. In order to do so, it is necessary to realize that:

> **Good anticipation is the result of good strategic exploration.**

With strategic exploration, you can discover the possible futures, and, once you have found out what is possible, you are in position to anticipate it.

There are five components to strategic exploration:

1. **Influence understanding**—the ability to be able to understand what influences your perceptions as you set out on your explorations.

2. **Divergent thinking**—the thinking skills necessary for discovering more than one right answer.

3. **Convergent thinking**—the thinking skills that allow the focused integration of the data and the prioritizing of choices.

4. **Mapping**—the capacity to draw pathways to show you how to get from the present to the future.

5. **Imaging**—the ability to picture in words or drawings or models what you found in your explorations of the future.

The complete strategic explorer can do all of these things.

This book focuses on the first component, **influence understanding**. Because if you don't understand how your perceptions of the future are influenced, all the other components are useless.

The ability to anticipate comes as a result of good strategic exploration. Some anticipation can be scientific, but the most important aspect of anticipation is artistic. And, just like the artist, practice and persistence will dramatically improve your abilities. Your improved ability will, in turn, increase your ability in dealing with the new worlds coming.

"It's twenty cents, isn't it?"

CHAPTER 3

Defining a Paradigm

WHEN I BEGAN TALKING about paradigms in 1974 to corporate audiences, a lot of people asked me why I was wasting my time with such a strange idea. Most people didn't even know how to pronounce the word, much less define it.

Most of the changes on the list in Chapter 2 were driven by a special phenomenon—a switch in paradigms (pronounced pair-a-dimes). And, in the jargon of futurists, they would be called "paradigm shifts."

The concept of paradigms and paradigm shifts can help you better understand the nature of those unexpected changes described in Chapter 2. Being able to understand what caused them will give you a better chance to anticipate other paradigm shifts.

Today, "paradigm" is a buzzword and people use it loosely. But it is not a loose idea.

What is a paradigm? If you look up the word in the dictionary, you discover that it comes from the Greek *paradeigma,* which means "model, pattern, example."

Let me give you some definitions that have appeared in various books since 1962. Thomas S. Kuhn, a scientific historian, and author of *The Structure of Scientific Revolutions* brought the concept of the paradigm to the scientific world. Kuhn wrote that scientific paradigms are "accepted examples of actual scientific practice, examples which include law, theory, application, and instrumentation together—[that] provide models from which spring particular coherent traditions of scientific research." He adds: "Men whose research is based on shared paradigms are committed to the same rules and standards for scientific practice" (page 10).

Adam Smith's definition, in his *Powers of the Mind,* is: "A shared set of assumptions. The paradigm is the way we perceive the world; water to the fish. The paradigm explains the world to us and helps us to predict its behavior." Smith's point about prediction is important. We will see that most of the time we do not predict things with our paradigms. But paradigms do give us the added advantage of being able to create a valid set of expectations about what will probably occur in the world based on our shared set of assumptions. "When we are in the middle of the paradigm," Smith concludes, "it is hard to imagine any other paradigm" (page 19).

In *An Incomplete Guide to the Future,* Willis Harmon, who was one of the key leaders at the Stanford Research Institute, writes that a paradigm is "the basic way of perceiving, thinking, valuing, and doing associated with a particular vision of reality. A dominant paradigm is seldom if ever stated explicitly; it exists as unquestioned, tacit understanding that is transmitted through culture and to succeeding generations through direct experience rather than being taught.''

In *The Aquarian Conspiracy*, Marilyn Ferguson, who first made her name as editor and publisher of the *New Sense Bulletin*, writes: ''A paradigm is a framework of thought . . . a scheme for understanding and explaining certain aspects of reality'' (page 26).

Let me offer my definition:

> **A paradigm is a set of rules and regulations (written or unwritten) that does two things: (1) it establishes or defines boundaries; and (2) it tells you how to behave inside the boundaries in order to be successful.**

And how do you measure success?

For most situations success is easily measured by your ability to solve problems, problems from trivial to profound. If you think about that definition, you should immediately get a sense of how widely it could be applied. For example: Based on my definition, is the game of tennis a paradigm? If you think about it for a minute, you'll discover that it is. Does the game of tennis have boundaries? Of course, that's the easy part. The tricky part has to do with success and problem solving. What is the problem in tennis? It's the ball coming over the net. And you must solve that problem according to the rules of tennis.

You must hit the problem with a tennis racket; not a baseball bat or your hand or your foot. And if you hit it back over the net so that it drops inside the boundaries on the other side, you have solved the problem. And your successful solution becomes your opponent's problem. In a very real sense you and your opponent exchange problems until one of you offers the other a problem that he or she cannot solve. Tennis is a paradigm. All games are paradigms. The beauty of games is that the boundaries are so clearly defined and the requirements for winning—problem solving—are so specific. Games allow for clear winners and losers. It is that aspect that generates much of any game's attraction. It is also that aspect that greatly disconnects them from reality.

Let us look at more important paradigms. Like your field of expertise. Almost everyone has one, either at work or at home. You may be an engineer, or a salesperson, or a chef or a carpenter or a nurse or an economist. Are these paradigms?

Again, let us apply the test. What does the word "field" suggest? Boundaries. How do you feel when you are outside your field? Not competent, right? Not competent to do what? Solve problems. Why do people come to you? To receive help from you in solving problems in your field. That sounds like paradigms, doesn't it?

Do artists have paradigms? I used to tease and say artists were just wild and crazy folks. Then I got straightened out by an artist. She came up after one of my speeches and said, "I'm a sculptor. What do you think the piece of marble I work with is?" I saw that it was her "field" and then I realized she was going to work "inside the field" by chiseling into that block of marble.

"Okay," I said to her, "but you can do anything you want with that piece of marble."

"Not if I want to be judged successful," she retorted. And then she told me of the rules of "texture" and "form" and "balance" and "content" that she had to follow in order to be considered successful.

Since that encounter, I have begun to listen to artists talk, especially about the "problems" they have solved in their work, whether it is a problem of perspective, or of color, or of tonality, or of character development. Artists have paradigms.

In a sense, I am constructing a hierarchy. At the top sits science and technology. That's where Thomas Kuhn focused. Science and technology deserve top billing because they are so careful with their paradigms, in terms of writing them down, and of developing measurement devices of increasing precision to tell whether they have solved a particular problem.

And, once a scientist has performed a successful experiment, it is expected that he or she should be able to hand the notes and the apparatus to another scientist who should then be able to replicate that experiment, getting the same results.

We would never expect a tennis player to be able to "replicate" Boris Becker's serve by just reading his notes and using the same tennis racket. Or someone to replicate an artist's work by being given the same pigments, paintbrushes, and canvas. The requirement of reproducibility constitutes a very important difference between science and all other fields. It results in science and its technologies having much more power to manipulate reality. But, even though they are more powerful, if you apply the definition I offered to science and technology, you will see that it holds true.

Over the years, I have collected words that represent subsets of the paradigm concept. Below they are ordered on a spectrum ranging from challengeable to unchallengeable. You may disagree with my arrangement, but take a look at the words and think about the boundaries and rules and regulations for success that are implicit in them.

Theory

Model

Methodology

Principles

Standards

Protocol

Routines

Assumptions

Conventions

Patterns

Habits

Common Sense

Conventional Wisdom

Mind-set

Values

Frames of Reference

Traditions

Customs

Prejudices

Ideology

Inhibitions

Superstitions

Rituals

Compulsions

Addictions

Doctrine

Dogma

Please note that nowhere in the list do the words "culture," "worldview," "organization," or "business" appear. That is because cultures, worldviews, organizations, and businesses are forests of paradigms. IBM is not one paradigm; it is a collection of many. That is true for any business. Large or small, they have management paradigms, sales paradigms, recruitment paradigms, marketing paradigms, research and development paradigms, human resource development paradigms. It goes on but I am sure you get the point. And there are even more paradigms in our cultural life: how we raise our children; how we deal with sex; how we define honesty; the foods we eat, the music we listen to.

And the interrelationship of all these paradigms is crucial to the success and longevity of any culture or organization. That is captured in the word "forest"—a highly interdependent structure. As we know from the environmental paradigm, when one thing in the forest is altered, it affects everything else there. So when someone within your organization starts messing with their paradigm and says, "Don't worry, it's got nothing to do with you," start worrying. It is never just one paradigm that is changed.

A paradigm, in a sense, tells you that there is a game, what the game is, and how to play it successfully. The idea of a game is a very appropriate metaphor for paradigms because it reflects the need for borders and directions on how to perform correctly. A paradigm tells you how to play the game according to the rules.

> **A paradigm shift, then, is a change to a new game, a new set of rules.**

It is my belief that changes in paradigms are behind much of society's turbulence during the last thirty years. We had sets of rules we knew well, then someone changed the rules. We understood the old boundaries, then we had to learn new boundaries. And those changes dramatically upset our world.

In *Megatrends,* the best-seller of 1982, John Naisbitt reflects in an indirect way how important paradigm shifts are. Naisbitt suggested that there were ten important new trends that would generate profound changes in our society in the next fifteen to thirty years.

I believe that if you look for what initiated those trends, you will find a paradigm shift. What Naisbitt identifies for us in *Megatrends* is important, because he shows us a pathway of change that we can follow through time to measure how we are getting more of something or less of something.

But, even more important than the pathway is our understanding of what instigated that change in the first place. We almost always find that at the beginning of the trend, someone created a new set of rules. The trend toward decentralization is an excellent example of a paradigm shift. The old rules, the old game, required that we "centralize the organization and make the hierarchy complex." But that game ultimately created big problems. Then somebody discovered that there was a different way to deal with the problems, which was to decentralize the organization and simplify the structure; in other words, to change the rules. The result was a paradigm shift.

So if you want to improve your ability to anticipate the future, don't wait for the trends to develop. Instead, **watch for people messing with the rules, because that is the earliest sign of significant change.**

FOUR QUESTIONS

One of the difficulties I have with Thomas Kuhn's *Structure of Scientific Revolutions* is his insistence that paradigms exist only in science. In his Afterword, Kuhn takes great pains to talk about all other disciplines as being "preparadigmatic" because they do not have the exactness of science. And yet, again and again I saw the phenomena he writes about in nonscientific settings and situations. Then I realized that a key element in one of his most powerful examples was not scientific but cultural—a simple deck of cards. The cards were used in a scientific experiment to prove that people have great difficulty perceiving "red" spades and ''black'' hearts when they are intermixed with standard cards and flashed very quickly at an observer. But even though the experiment was scientific, the objects of the experiment, the cards, are cultural artifacts. And the expectations about the correct colors are cultural expectations, not scientific expectations.

So the experiment was actually a measure of the power of a simple cultural paradigm—the card-deck paradigm—to set up boundaries that dramatically influenced the way the subjects of the experiment saw the anomalous cards.

I am convinced that what Thomas Kuhn discovered about paradigms is a description not just of science but of the human condition.

When we look back to the 1960s, we see nonscientific paradigm shifts: Parents responded so violently to drugs and long hair on their children because these things represented a cultural paradigm shift; we missed the OPEC revolution because of an economic paradigm shift. Our country's inability to understand the Iranian revolution had to do with religious paradigms. Much of the confusion we have about the future is because of changes in paradigms.

These paradigm changes are especially important for all of us because, whether it is in business or education or politics or our personal lives, a paradigm change, by definition, alters the basic rules of the game.

> **And, when the rules change, the whole world can change.**

The points that Kuhn makes about scientific paradigm shifts are true for any situation where strongly held rules and regulations exist.

I should also add the following disclaimer: I doubt very much if Kuhn appreciates the extent to which I, and others, have generalized his concepts. In his book he states that only in science, where the rules and examples and measures are precise, can paradigms exist. He also contends that only with the subtlety and accuracy possessed by science can changes in paradigms be measured so as to trigger the search for a new paradigm. I accept the obligation imposed by Kuhn's own careful qualification. In spite of his argument to the contrary, I still believe that his observations can be applied in a broader sense with great utility. I hope you will find this true as well.

To frame this broader discussion, we will ask four questions about paradigms:

1. When do new paradigms appear? This question is all about timing. If we can know when the new rules are going to show up, then we can anticipate our future with much greater accuracy. Timing may not be everything, but it's a great place to start.

2. What kind of person is a paradigm shifter? It is as important to understand who are the paradigm shifters, the people who change the rules, as it is to know when they show up. Of the four kinds of paradigm shifters that will be described, three are already inside your organization. But typically, we do not understand how to use them to our advantage. In fact, we usually are very hard on these people.

3. Who are the early followers of the paradigm shifters and why do they follow them? I call these people paradigm pioneers. Without them, paradigm shifts take much longer. Paradigm pioneers bring the critical mass of brainpower and effort and key resources necessary to drive the new rules into reality. Very few of us can be paradigm shifters; many more of us, if we understand our roles, can be paradigm pioneers.

4. How does a paradigm shift affect those who go through it? It is crucial to answer this last question if we are going to understand why there is so much resistance to new paradigms. It also explains the great gulf between old and new paradigm practitioners.

When we have answered these four questions, we will have identified the Paradigm Principles.

CHAPTER 4

When Do New Paradigms Appear?

LET ME begin answering the first question by drawing a graph that describes the life span of a paradigm. To verify this graph, I visited people with specific paradigms, scientific, technological, organizational, social. I showed them the "curve" and asked them to describe each aspect of the curve using their own paradigm to illustrate. Everyone, without exception, was able to do it.

First let's label the axes in Figure 2: The horizontal or X axis will represent **Time.** So as we move to the right, time is passing. The vertical or Y axis represents **Problems Solved** using the prevailing paradigm. Therefore, each point represents a new problem solved at a specific time.

The process starts, not at zero, but up a little bit where the star is on the Y axis. Someone solves a couple of problems in a funny way—that is, they don't use the old rules to do it.

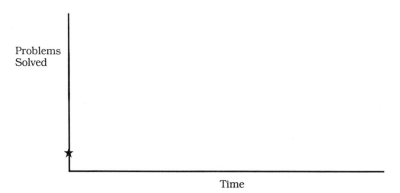

Problems
Solved

Time

Figure 2

They say to themselves, "Gee, I didn't know I could do it that way."

Then they say, "Maybe I've got something here!" This expression can be translated into, "Maybe I've found hiding in these solutions, a way of solving a lot more problems than these three or four I just solved. Maybe I have a new pattern, a new model, a new system for solving a huge array of problems." And that is the start! Kuhn called these special categories of solutions "exemplars."

Now look at Phase A of development (Figure 3). Look at how flat the line is. Remember that this line is made of dots representing solved problems. Can you see how slowly we are progressing? Typically, the response during this time to the person with the new idea is, "Hey, I thought you said you had something!" Where are all the solved problems?

Why isn't the new paradigm solving problems rapidly? That's what everyone expects. It looked promising, but where's the payoff? The answer is simple: It is a long and tricky way from "Maybe I've got something" to knowing, with precision, the

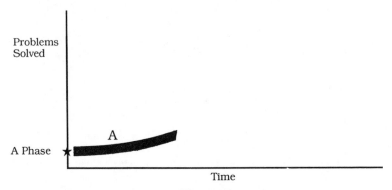

Figure 3

rules and regulations of a new paradigm. Exactly how big are the boundaries? You have to do a lot of work just to begin to find out. What are the most efficient rules for solving the problems inside those boundaries? It takes time and effort to refine the answers to those two questions.

Note that there is a **slight** slope to the A phase. Problems are being solved, but usually only to identify more clearly the boundaries and to refine the problem-solving rules. Until you have those rules well understood, you can't begin rapid problem solving. That will come in the second phase (Figure 4).

If you are successful in Phase A at identifying the new rules, then Phase B follows. The dramatic change in the angle of the curve in Phase B indicates that you understand the paradigm. You have become efficient at finding problems that can be solved using the new paradigm and effective at applying the rules to discover solutions.

Now there is rapid problem solving. Now are the good times. Now are the moneymaking opportunities. Now, during Phase B, is when whole new industries develop.

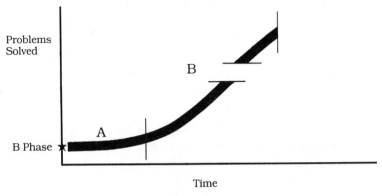

Figure 4

We are currently seeing exactly this kind of rapid growth in the environmental industries. It was in the early 1960s that some-one first said, "Gee, maybe it would be a good idea to keep the air and water and soil clean." We spent a lot of time figuring out how to do that. Now we are in the B phase. In the 1990s we are in the midst of applying the new environmental paradigm and companies like Waste Management, Inc. are growing explosively because of it.

The videotape recorder has exactly the same history. In-vented in the United States by Ampex, the initial models weighed more than one hundred pounds and cost $250,000. The Japanese then took this idea in the A phase and worked out the systems and practices needed to drive it out of A and into the B phase of development where they could economically apply this new par-adigm to the problems of entertainment and education.

You'll notice a break in the B segment of the line. Every paradigm has a range of problems it can solve. The more pow-erful the paradigm, the more problems it will solve over time. That is why we honor science so much. Scientific paradigms tend to be broad in their reach and long-lived because of that. Think about quantum physics—it is almost ninety years since Einstein did the initial mathematics and it is still going strong.

Yet there have been marketing paradigms that lived only a couple of years, because their problem set was very small.

Let's take a look at the C phase of the Paradigm Curve shown in Figure 5. We see the rate of problem solving begin to slow down, and the number of problems solved diminish. The time between problems solved increases.

What's happening? Are we getting dumber? Not at all. As we climb higher on the curve, the problems remaining typically increase in their difficulty, for good reason. We have solved all the simpler ones. It is human nature that people will solve the easy problems first, especially if they are getting paid for solving problems. Harder problems take longer to solve, cost more to solve, give you less chance to demonstrate how good a problem solver you are so we set them aside. By the time we get

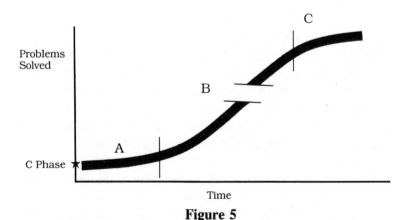

Figure 5

to the C phase, all that remains are the toughest, most sophisticated problems of the paradigm. Of course, each will take longer to solve.

There it is—the Paradigm Curve. It is a simple but useful way to depict the life-span of a paradigm. The classic S-shaped curve. And it makes perfect sense: Slow in the A phase because we don't know the rules well enough to be good at application. Fast in the B phase because we now know how to play the game, and there is a large inventory of problems waiting to be solved. Slow in the C phase because all we have left are the most difficult problems.

Now let us ask our first question about the curve: **Where on the curve is the likely location for the next paradigm to appear?** The logical answer is, somewhere in Phase C. After all, the need is clear; the costs are dear; the fear of not being able to solve any more problems becomes a rational driving force.

But, surprise, the new paradigm usually shows up much earlier—in Phase B. For most people, that is unexpected. It doesn't make sense. And yet as soon as you understand the driving forces, it is perfectly logical.

When we look at that location in Figure 6, we could also say, "the new paradigm appears sooner than it is needed." And from that follows, "Sooner than it is wanted." Given both of those statements, what do you suppose is the logical and rational response to the new paradigm the first time it is offered?

Rejection, of course. Because those practicing the prevailing paradigm can make a wonderful case for that rejection. How have they been doing? Great! What is the trend of their success?

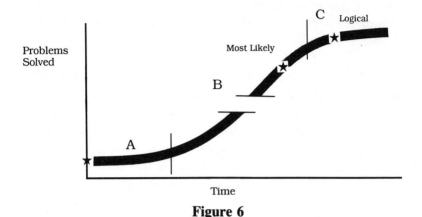

Figure 6

Ever upward! What are their expectations for the future based on past performance? Even greater!

So, when the new paradigm shows up in Phase B, it has a very difficult time being accepted.

> **Knowing when a new paradigm shows up is useful because it makes you start watching sooner than you would otherwise.**

WHAT CAUSES A PARADIGM TO SHIFT?

In order to really gain some leverage from the ''when'' question, we need to know what the initiating factors that cause new paradigms to be discovered are, and why they show up so early. Here we turn directly to Thomas Kuhn's work (page 84) because he provides us with an explanation that will lead us to significant clues for anticipating our own future. (See Figure 7.)

Let us start by asking this: As we work our way up the B segment of the line, do we solve 100 percent of the problems we attack?

The answer is no. However, we don't expect perfection, just a high enough success ratio to feel confident about our paradigm. So, while we are not batting 1.000, we are doing very well, thank you.

And what do we do with the problems we don't solve? We put them aside, up on a shelf, so to speak. And we make a promise to ourselves, "We'll get back to them sooner or later."

Kuhn explained that in science there are two good reasons why these problems aren't solved right away. It turns out all of us, scientists or not, have these same reasons.

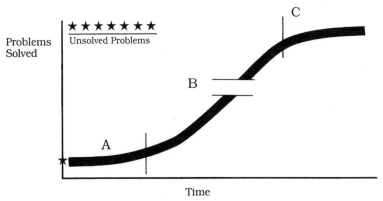

Figure 7

Reason 1. We lack some technology or tool that would allow us to be able to solve the problem. For instance, until accountants got a new computer software tool called Visicalc, there was a whole set of problems that had to do with rapid calculation of extensive spread sheets that couldn't be done. Before Visicalc, the recalculation would have taken weeks or even months, depending on the size. So such problems just weren't solved. But then Visicalc showed up—a new tool. These "extensive calculation" problems came down off the shelf because now it was a simple matter of a couple of key strokes and the software did the rest.

Another example: Until we had Boeing 707s and atomic clocks, we could not perform certain tests on Einstein's theory of relativity measuring how time was affected by speed. Once we had those two tools, we could and did. (The results indicated Einstein was right.)

Reason 2. We're not smart enough yet. Sometimes you run into a problem that is too sophisticated for you. It isn't lack of tools, it's your inability to use the paradigm in sophisticated ways. So you must wait on certain problems until you can "play the game" better. It's like a good tennis player with solid forehand and backhand shots, but no court sense. Getting better at the game will allow that player to deal with certain shots that at his present level of skill are impossible to return.

We all are capable of solving problems today we could not have dealt with four years ago. This is exactly the kind of maturation Kuhn was talking about. You just get better at using the paradigm.

Both of these reasons put the burden of solving the problem not on the paradigm—it is assumed it will work—but on the application of our skills and the development of new tools. This is totally valid. Again and again, problems come off the shelf to be solved by the power of the prevailing paradigm, as shown in Figure 8.

But a small subset of problems do **not** come off the shelf. The new tools are developed; they don't help. The paradigm practitioners get wiser, cleverer; it doesn't help.

> **And sooner or later, every paradigm begins to develop a very special set of problems that everyone in the field wants to be able to solve and no one has a clue as to how to do it.**

How are those special problems going to be solved?

By changing paradigms.

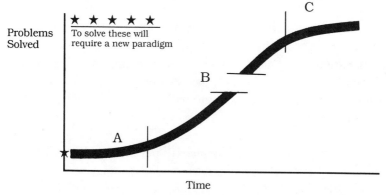

Figure 8

Let me put it another way:

> **Every paradigm will, in the process of finding new problems, uncover problems it cannot solve. And those unsolvable problems provide the catalyst for triggering the paradigm shift.**

The implications of this are significant. It means that each paradigm identifies the beacons to the next paradigm. Yet, unless you are sensitive to these signals, you will make a perfectly rational mistake: You will assume that sooner or later the paradigm you are presently practicing (which has been mostly successful) will solve **all** the rest of your problems. It seems only a matter of enough time and money.

So the successful practitioners of the prevailing paradigm hold on to their model far past when they should have begun exploring for a new one. And that is why Phase C seems to be the right place for the new paradigm to show up. It is actually the time we recognize our need for a new paradigm.

It is possible for new paradigms to appear at any point along the curve. When it happens during the A phase, it is usually in competition with other paradigms in development. Whichever paradigm makes it to the turn, the beginning of B, almost always wins. Even if the other paradigm will solve more problems over the long haul.

The reason is simple: People will put their money down on an idea that is working rather than an idea that may be better but hasn't proved itself. Plus, solving those early problems within the new boundaries can make a lot of money.

Then the better paradigm has to wait for the less effective paradigm to run out of problems it can solve thus triggering the search for the next paradigm.

New paradigms sometimes wait until C to get developed. But this kind of delay is usually caused by artificial barriers to exploration: government regulation; a distorted marketplace; an oligopoly that crushes anyone venturing onto its turf.

But if you want to play the probabilities, you should look to late B because by then there will be enough special problems "on the shelf" to trigger the search.

How can you explicitly identify the problems on your paradigm shelf? Simply ask yourself: **In my own specialty or field of expertise, what are the problems that all my peers want to solve and we don't have the slightest idea of how to do it?** Write them down. When you do, you are identifying the problems on your shelf. Having this information can be very useful as you will see in the next chapter.

Let me give you a nonscientific example of how a set of these problems plague a paradigm. The legal field has a shelf full of seemingly insoluble problems that has grown to impressive size over the past few years. Here are just three problems from that shelf that look as if they have no solutions within the prevailing paradigm:

- A turtle-slow movement of cases through the court systems coupled to repeated rounds of appeals. Justice delayed by endless routines.

- The cost of defense. Only the well-off can afford to defend themselves adequately. How can that be justice?

- An ongoing pattern of no negotiations except in the courts with all-or-nothing strategies and gigantic settlement requests.

Yet most lawyers would have perfectly valid explanations for these problems. They would suggest that while these problems are troublesome, they will not force a fundamental change in the system.

One last question about the curve: *Where are you, on this curve?* When I ask this question of my audiences, almost everyone can locate themselves: Are you just starting to develop a new way of solving problems? Then you are in A. Are you in the middle of B? Then I would expect you to be solving problems with efficiency and effectiveness. Are you in C? Then your problems are very subtle and sophisticated. Also expensive and extensive.

Knowing your location on the curve, or your department's, or your industry's, helps you think about your future and gives you important indicators for anticipating the future.

So, paradigms, by their nature, uncover and identify problems they will never solve. It is through this ongoing process that the stage is set for a paradigm shift. The seeds of succession are sown and begin to germinate even while the prevailing paradigm is still vigorous. The critical mass is put in place and awaits the "paradigm shifter."

Who Changes the Paradigm?

NOW WE UNDERSTAND the structure of the curve. We understand that the new paradigm is going to be driven by unsolved problems on the "shelf" of the prevailing paradigm. We also understand that the new paradigm has a high likelihood of appearing while the prevailing paradigm is still performing admirably.

So who changes the paradigm?

The short and unsettling answer is that it will probably be someone who is **an outsider**. Someone who really doesn't understand the prevailing paradigm in all its subtleties (sometimes they don't understand it at all!).

In *Structure of Scientific Revolutions*, Kuhn identified two categories of paradigm shifters. I have identified a rare third and an interesting fourth category. You will recognize these kinds of people in whatever your field of endeavor. They are archetypes of change agents.

Before I describe these paradigm shifters in greater detail, we need to stop and examine a dilemma they create by merely being outsiders. These people are bringing you your future. And yet, as outsiders, what is their credibility? Zero, right? They can't begin to understand what you are doing and yet here they are telling you to change the fundamentals of what you are so good at!

Who do they think they are? To put them in their place we have a whole set of phrases to use when they come to show us their great new idea. Try a few of these on for size:

"That's impossible."

"We don't do things that way around here."

"It's too radical a change for us."

"We tried something like that before and it didn't work."

"I wish it were that easy."

"It's against policy to do it that way."

"When you've been around a little longer, you'll understand."

"Who gave you permission to change the rules?"

"Let's get real, okay?"

"How dare you suggest that what we are doing is wrong!"

And the classic response from the wizened veteran to the new person:

"If you had been in this field as long as I have, you would understand that what you are suggesting is absolutely absurd!"

Something as absurd as using ceramic materials for super-conductors (which resulted in a Nobel Prize). Or making rolled steel in very small mills out of scrap metal (which changed the basic economies of the steel industry). Or building a useful computer so cheap that anyone could afford to have one on his desk. . . . well, you get the point. What may sound absurd may be the birth of a new industry, the start of a whole new field of study, the beginning of a revolution.

Keep in mind that when people respond harshly to outsiders, their responses can be justified. People who have been practicing the prevailing paradigm have been successful. Nothing in their situation says they need to change. They still are ascending the problem-solving curve. All the signals, based on their own hard work, say they are right. So, of course, they have a difficult time listening to outsiders who ask them to change their ways.

Let's take a look at the four categories of paradigm shifters.

Category 1: A young person fresh out of training. He or she has studied the paradigm but never practiced in it. And we all know the difference between those two situations. "Let me show you how we **really** do that around here," we say to the trainee. And "how we do it" is usually much better than the way the trainee was taught. After all, our techniques have been tested in the real world. I am not being facetious about this; the skills brought about through practice are almost always cleverer, better ways to apply the paradigm.

Albert Einstein represents this kind of youthful innocence in science. Fred Smith, founder of Federal Express, was this person in the field of overnight package delivery. Steve Jobs and Steve Wozniak did it with their Apple computers. It's easy to find lots of examples of just this sort of paradigm shifter by examining the entrepreneurial ranks.

Category 2: An older person shifting fields. (This is good news for all of us over forty!) Being a paradigm shifter is **not** a function of age. A person in this category may have been, probably was, an expert in another field of endeavor: a chemist, a marketing person, an English teacher. Then, for some reason, this person decided to change to a totally unrelated field.

Dr. Alex Mueller, Nobel Prize cowinner in 1987, is a perfect example. He was a physicist with a well-established reputation but not in superconducting. In a *Wall Street Journal* article on August 19, 1987, Dr. Mueller said: "I was a greenhorn and an outsider in the specialized field of superconducting."

W. Edwards Deming, the guru of the Total Quality movement, is another example of an outsider, a statistician, who has made a monumental impact on the field of manufacturing. And at an age when most of us would be happy just to be alive, he is charging around Planet Earth teaching all who will listen. Clearly an older outsider.

Bill Weimer, formerly with IBM, got his degree in physics, went through a series of field changes from systems engineer to marketing for IBM in California, then switched from marketing to take over the technical education effort for GSD, a division of IBM, in the late 1970s. Five years later he had created, with no budget and virtually no head count, a fundamentally new way to find, train, and motivate teachers inside the organization.

Weimer ultimately had more than two hundred people working for him and a budget in excess of $30 million. And still no official head count or budget. His techniques and ideas are now beginning to reach the rest of the corporate world. He also illustrates perfectly the power of the older outsider shifting fields.

Let's stop for a minute to examine what advantages these two categories of people have in common. First, they both share **operational naïveté** about the fields they have just entered. They don't understand many of the subtler aspects of the paradigm community they want to be part of. Second, they don't know what **can't** be done. Why is that an advantage? Very simply, if you don't know you can't achieve something, sometimes you do it.

It turns out that the great advantage these people have is a special kind of ignorance. Or more softly put, a kind of innocence. They ask "dumb" questions. They wonder about behaviors and approaches that are accepted by those "in the know." They don't realize they shouldn't challenge the present practices because they haven't learned those prohibitions yet.

And, please notice, you know exactly who these people are in your organization. You hire them. You transfer them. But, how do we perceive their value when they show up? Zero. Until we train them, "bring them up to speed," "show them the ropes," indoctrinate them. Then, and only then, do we think they will be useful to the organization.

Well, guess what. **As soon as you've "brought them up to speed," you've lost a resource!**

Let me make a suggestion: Remember that shelf of unsolved problems from your present paradigm that I asked you to write down in the last chapter? Now, let's use that list and the innocence of our new outsiders.

The first thing you should do when they show up is give them some of those problems. One is not enough because you can't find a pattern in a set of one. Ten or fifteen is too many because you scare them to death. Somewhere in the range of three to six is appropriate. Give your new people these problems and ask them to begin immediately working on their solution. Make an appointment to meet with them in the next week or ten days.

Then go easy on the training.

Give them a chance **not** to do it the "correct" way (which hasn't worked anyway). Now, in order to make this successful, you have to cut a deal with all the people in your department or unit or group. No one may tell the newcomers that the problems you gave them are impossible to solve. If they do, the newcomers will think you are playing a joke on them and you will not get authentic effort.

Will this work? What's the likelihood that new person will bring back a paradigm shift? Zero again, right? Okay, let's be realistic: one person in a hundred at best, one in a thousand is more likely.

Then is it a waste of time? No. Because the value of that one in a thousand is enormous. And what's more, while you are working your way through to the big breakthrough, you as manager are learning two very important skills—how to listen outside the boundaries and how to reinforce your people for taking risks. By doing that, you establish an atmosphere conducive to exploration that will always pay off in the end.

Here are two stories to illustrate this principle: One is based on hearsay; the other is based on actual practice.

In the 1930s, the General Electric Company supposedly had a practical joke that it played on every new engineer in its incandescent lighting group. It went like this: Each new engineer began his job by meeting with the director of the division. The director would turn on an incandescent light bulb and observe, "Do you see the hot spot in this bulb." (In those days you could almost see the filament even though the bulb had a coating on it.) "Your job is to develop a new coating that smooths that illumination out so that the entire surface of the bulb glows in a uniform manner."

With the assignment clear, the young engineer would go off to tackle this problem. What everybody knew was that it couldn't be done. After several weeks of struggle the new engineer would admit defeat and then, to the hearty laughs of his colleagues who had also failed, he would be told of the impossibility of his task.

And it was a good joke, an illuminating initiation rite, until around 1952, when a newly hired engineer returned to the director, screwed his bulb into the socket, and turned it on. "Is this what you were looking for, sir?" he asked. And, as the director looked at the first bulb that met his impossible conditions, he reportedly said, "Ah, yup. That's it."

The tradition had ended. The joke was finished. The initiation rite was dead. And a new way to coat the inside of light bulbs had been created.

What GE was doing, if this story is true, was accidentally wise. It was engaging the innocence of the new people to look for solutions to problems that the older engineers didn't have a clue how to solve. I have never been able to check out this story for its veracity. But the next one I know to be true.

In the late 1980s, I gave a series of lectures for the Marriott Corporation. One of them was for the general managers of the hotels. I talked about using the new people to solve impossible problems. Then in the spring of 1990, I was visiting another consultant, at a Marriott hotel in Burlington, north of Boston.

As I walked in, the general manager recognized me. Excited, he called me over. "Joel," he said. "Remember when you told us about using our new people to come up with breakthrough ideas?"

I nodded and then he told me this story: When he returned from that meeting, he decided to test my recommendation. He began to go to the first meetings of the new trainees.

There he made the following comments to each group (which I will paraphrase):

"You are my new eyes and ears. In the next couple of weeks you are going to see strange things here. We will be doing things you know how to do much better. You will see ways of solving problems that will be very different from the way we are solving them now.''

Then he invited them to visit him in his office to tell him about their ideas. He set aside time every afternoon especially for that purpose.

With that, he left. What do you think happened? He told me he had had more good suggestions in the six months from the inception of this approach than he had in the last six years.

And, furthermore, the success of these new, uninitiated people, had been so surprising to the older staff that, out of pride, they were now coming in to visit him with their ideas on how to do things better.

What is going on here? It's very simple: We are using the power of **lack of knowledge** coupled with human creativity. The old rules maintained that you couldn't make a contribution until you knew enough. Wrong. You can make significant contributions at any time.

Category 3: The maverick. This is a person who **is** an insider, a practitioner of the prevailing paradigm who sees the problems on the shelf, understands that the present paradigm will not work to solve them, and leads the charge to change paradigms.

These people exist but they tend to work at the fringes of their disciplines. They are known as mavericks, as hard cases, as the people who are always asking questions, as wild ducks. And, almost without exception, these people are not welcomed until there is a crisis.

> **Their advantage is that they are knowledgeable about the paradigm but not captured by it.**

These people exist but they are rare. Twice in Motorola's history, the Galvin at the top played this role: first Paul Galvin, founder of Motorola, in developing car radios when radios were huge clunky receivers that sat in the living room, and then Robert Galvin, his son, who took Motorola out of consumer electronics and into the manufacture of integrated chips, one of the most competitive arenas in the world. Both father and son knew the old paradigm but were not afraid to break the rules to make their company successful.

At 3M in St. Paul, Minnesota, the adhesive tape group created a cellulose tape that dominated the market, then, when their patent ran out, introduced a new paradigm—Magic Mending tape—and redominated the market.

In both cases, these behaviors were unusual in that each company was able to drive the paradigm shift from within rather than its being driven from without.

Every company needs such rule breakers at crucial junctures. Very few get them—or, if they have them, know how to use them.

Category 4: Tinkerers. Thomas Kuhn never recognized this category of people even though they exist in scientific and technological fields.

A tinkerer is a person who has run into one of those special problems on the paradigm's shelf. Tinkerers don't know it's a special problem, only that it is their problem. It is irrelevant to them that it is one of a set of important unsolved problems of some paradigm. They just know that this particular problem is in their way and their life really can't go on properly until they solve it.

So they start to work on their problem. Most tinkerers fail, because these problems are tough. But, every once and a while, they solve their single problem. And inadvertently they create through their solution a special example that leads to a model, a theory, an approach—a paradigm—for solving an entire class of problems.

Look who revolutionized accounting by developing the electronic spread sheet? Some Arthur Andersen expert? A veteran from Ernst & Young? A full professor from the Harvard Business School? Wrong! It was a young computer programmer who knew precious little about accounting. But he did have this idea that he could make his little Apple computer do some pretty tricky adding and subtracting that might be useful to accountants. So he wrote a program called Visicalc, and as he created it, he kept an accounting textbook beside him to make sure he was doing it right. A clear case of a tinkerer.

The Bell telephone system was revolutionized in the late nineteenth century by a tinkerer. His name was Almond B. Strowger and he invented and patented the switching system that took the operator out of the day-to-day loop of making connections.

His profession: Undertaker. Mortician. Funeral director.

Can you think of anyone more unlikely to revolutionize the most sophisticated technology of the day? And yet he had his reasons, all brought about by the advent of the telephone in Kansas City, where he lived. What he noticed was that the more phones that were installed in his city, the lower his business went. Previously, he had a nice 50 percent of the city's undertaking work. Now it was dropping precipitously. He had a problem. He decided it must be the phones.

So he went to the phone company to talk to them about his problem. Of course, to us his reasoning was absurd. What possible connection could there be?

It turned out the connection was direct and dire. He discovered that the head operator, who trained all the other operators, was the wife of the one other undertaker in town. And guess how she trained "all her girls"? When someone asked for the undertaker, they were always connected to her husband.

So Mr. Strowger tried to discuss the problem. He suggested a way to return to the old percentages. She said no.

He went home with a much clearer understanding of his dilemma. After much thinking, he realized what he had to do: He had to figure out some way for telephone callers to get to him without going through the operators.

In 1888 he received his patents that led to automatic switching and rotary dialing. His solution to his problem was a solution to an enormous number of other problems. And even today, more than one hundred years later, many parts of the world still use the results of his tinkering.

So there we have it. Three kinds of insider/outsiders and one true outsider. All rare. All precious. All hard to find. When they show up, we usually treat them badly. We try to get them to be like the rest of us and then disparage them when they aren't. And yet, especially the insider/outsiders offer us a wonderful opportunity, because we know exactly who they are. If only we will listen.

But, too often, we don't. What usually happens is best illustrated by the following story:

I was lecturing at a famous research facility. We took a break just as I had finished talking about outsiders. A woman came up to me and said, "You need to say one more thing about outsiders. We are very fragile and break easily."

I agreed that it was a good point. Then I observed, "You said 'we.' What happened to you?" She shared the following story:

She had joined the company three years before. About a month after joining she had a "big" idea. "How big?" I asked. "Worth about five hundred million dollars," she answered.

She was very excited about the idea so she put together her notes and called the director. She said she would like to talk to him and he replied by telling her to come on up, because he "loved talking to his new people."

She said the first couple of minutes was friendly chitchat, getting-to-know-you kind of talk. Then, when there came the inevitable lull, she pulled out her notes and began presenting her idea.

She said that as she talked, the director became more and more agitated. After just a couple of minutes, he stood up from behind his desk, walked around it, picked up her notes, took her by the arm, and escorted her to the door.

At the door he said—and I quote her quoting him—"I hope you realize that if you had been here for five years I might continue listening to you." With that, he sent her on her way.

I commiserated with her. Then I asked what had happened to her idea. She said that a competitor had just announced a product that looked very much like her idea. "Ouch," I said. Then she made her closing comment and walked away.

What she said I will never forget: "I've had six ideas better than that one . . . but I haven't been here five years yet."

She and others like her who are smart enough to create revolutionary ideas are also smart enough to learn how to play the game. And the game at her company had, as one of its key rules, that you can't have a good idea until you have proven yourself over a time period of half a decade.

> **How soon can you have a good idea: the first day on the job. When's the latest you can have a great idea: your exit interview.**

To complete this discussion, we need to acknowledge one more reason for the resistance of the insider. It is the third major reason for rejection of new paradigms by insiders. It has to do with the investment the prevailing paradigm practitioners have made in their paradigms.

When paradigm shifters ask you to change, they are asking you to forsake your investment in the present paradigm. What has that investment given you?

1. The power to solve many important problems.

2. Your status among your peers as a problem solver.

3. Monetary remuneration (in many cases your salary is based on how well you use a paradigm).

4. Perhaps even your title and the corner office are the result of your facility in using your paradigm.

And here is this outsider asking you to abandon the very thing that gave you all these benefits. So when the outsider offers a new paradigm, the logical response is not, ''Oh, sure. Quick let me change.'' The more honest response is, ''Who the hell do you think you are?''

New paradigms put everyone practicing the old paradigm at great risk. The higher one's position, the greater the risk. The better you are at your paradigm, the more you have invested in it, the more you have to lose by changing paradigms.

But what have the outsiders invested in the prevailing paradigm? It is the same number as their credibility—zero. So what have they got to lose by creating a new paradigm? Nothing. And everything to gain. Until you appreciate this fact, you will misjudge the forces driving and blocking paradigm shifts.

The implications of these observations can be applied broadly. How often has an important innovation in technology, or business, or education, or any field that is doing well, come from the established practitioners? Rarely. Because if you are doing well using the old paradigm, it makes no sense to turn around and put yourself out of business by creating a new set of rules. It makes much more sense for you to continue to improve what you are already good at.

So where is the strange but logical place for innovation to come from? The edges. The fringes. Where there are outsiders who do not know that "it can't be done."

If there is any large theme to this discussion of outsiders I think it is the following:

> **You cannot know who is going to bring you your future. You cannot qualify them in advance by looking at degrees or experience, or gender or race. You can only listen.**

Unless you know what to listen for, all your rationality will tell you to reject the person and the idea.

You must have tolerance and patience. You must be open to surprise from the most unlikely of sources. Only then do you increase the likelihood that you will hear the paradigm shifters when first they speak. And it is hearing them the first time they speak that carries all the leverage.

CHAPTER 6

Who Are the Paradigm Pioneers?

WHAT'S THE DIFFERENCE between a pioneer and a settler? It is the settler who always is calling toward the horizon, "Is it safe out there now?" The voice calling back, "Of course, it's safe out here!" is the pioneer's. That is because the pioneers take the risk, go out early, and make the new territory safe.

These days, the pioneers will also ask, "Would you like to buy some land?"

It is paradigm pioneers who are first to follow the rough pathway that paradigm shifters have uncovered.

On the Paradigm Curve, the pioneers show up late in the A phase or very early in the B.

Without paradigm pioneers, paradigm shifts can falter, because paradigm pioneers bring the elements of brains, brawn, time, effort, and capital to create the critical mass which drives the new paradigm the remainder of the way through the A phase of the curve and into the B phase. (See Figure 9.)

The paradigm shifter has played the role of catalyst, of change agent, and has stirred up a lot of thinking in the prevailing paradigm community. The community acknowledges that the problems on their shelf should be solved. They know they are not solving them. They also know that the paradigm shifter has offered an alternative way of thinking about these difficult and important problems. Yet the community continues to defend the prevailing paradigm, because it is still very successful.

In the midst of this ambiguity, a few members of the prevailing paradigm community begin to assess the suggested new paradigm in an unusual way. You hear phrases like:

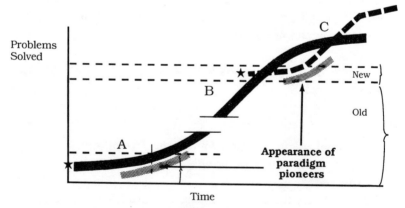

Figure 9

"You know, the more I examine these rules, rudimentary though they are, the more interesting they seem."

"There is something clever about the way these rules approach these intractable problems."

"I like the elegance of this approach."

"I don't know what it is, but there is something special going on here."

These musings reflect a kind of judgment being made about the new paradigm that is not quantitative but qualitative. An even better word to use is **intuitive**. There are many phrases for this kind of decision making: gut-level; seat-of-the-pants, from the heart, a gestalt. I like intuitive best. **Intuitive judgment: It is the ability to make good decisions with incomplete data.**

Thomas Kuhn identifies this kind of judgment as crucial to the early adopters of the new paradigm. According to Kuhn:

> The man who embraces a new paradigm at an early stage must often do so in defiance of the evidence provided by the problem solving. He must, that is, have faith that the new paradigm will succeed with the many large problems that confront it knowing only that the older paradigm has failed with a few. A decision of that kind can only be made **on faith** (pages 157–158, my emphasis).

If you ask paradigm pioneers to justify their decision to switch to a new paradigm, they can't do it using numbers. Because the numbers don't exist.

> **The essence of the pioneering decision is: Those who choose to change their paradigms early do it not as an act of the head but as an act of the heart.**

Captivated by a set of rules that suggests they may be able to succeed where before they failed, these pioneers risk their reputations, their positions, even their economic situations, on a nonrational decision. It is the aesthetic appeal of the new paradigm, the beauty with which it appears to solve problems, rather than quantitative proof of problem solving that precipitates the decision to change.

Driven by the frustration of the old and the appeal of the new, they cross the brink. They leap a professional chasm that separates the old paradigm, where the territory is well illuminated and where reputations and positions are clearly defined, into a new territory, illuminated by the new paradigm in such a limited way that it is impossible to know whether they are standing on the edge of an unexplored continent or merely on a tiny island.

Look at the curve again (Figure 9, page 72): How much evidence is there at that location to prove that changing to the new paradigm is a wise decision?

The answer is always the same: **Never Enough!**

Yet the pioneers switch, anyway. Why? How do they know they are making a correct decision? Can we be more explicit about this process beyond calling it intuitive?

After talking to many people who use this kind of decision-making process, I see a methodology. I believe that they are able to measure the rightness of the new pattern, the new model, by simulating the model's operation in their minds. They test the various alternative paradigms being presented, and through their mental modeling, identify the correct new paradigm out of several alternatives.

Those of us who cannot do this don't understand what is happening. It is this ability to run mental simulations that separates the true pioneers from the merely foolhardy who will try anything without proper judgment.

By identifying the new paradigm so early, the pioneers gain substantial advantage over their competition. That is the payoff for being a paradigm pioneer.

But intuition alone is not enough. We have all met people who, as the new paradigm gains visibility, say in condescending voices, "I knew all about that five years ago."

Their attitude grates on us. We want to ask, "Then why didn't you do something about it?"

They won't say, but the answer is simply, no guts. They lacked the courage to act on their intuition. So they were bystanders during the change, and are embittered because they didn't get in on the ground floor even though they knew it was coming.

The paradigm pioneer must have courage as well as intuition.

The major risk of paradigm pioneers is best illustrated by the line in Figure 10. They believe that the paradigm will solve many problems, but in fact, it is capable of solving only a few. They invested their time and reputation and money only to gain a few new problems solved.

That is what happened to the "tuning fork" watch, the Accutron, invented in the late 1950s and marketed in the early 1960s. Its pulse came from an electrically stimulated tuning fork that hummed at 360 cycles per second. The small vibration was translated via a series of mechanical levers to a geared wheel that drove the rest of the watch just like a standard mechanical watch. The 360 cycles was twelve times more accurate than a standard watch.

It looked like a powerful new way to improve watch accuracy. But the cost of manufacture was at least equal to that of a standard watch and it had many of the mechanical susceptibilities that limited its problem-solving performance. It could not compete with the huge new problem-solving potential

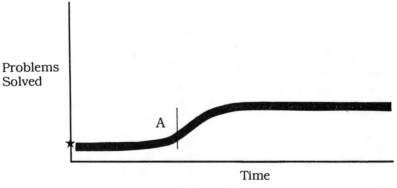

Figure 10

that the electronic timepiece, with its accuracy based on 30,000 cycles per second, had intrinsically. So the new paradigm of timekeeping became electronic not harmonic. Accutron was a limited paradigm.

But look at the advantage of paradigm pioneering when the correct decision is made. The United States pioneered environmental laws. Even when the rest of the world laughed at us for such unwise use of our assets, we proceeded to clean up the air and water. Now the rest of the world is moving to catch up with us.

Holiday Corporation (when they were still Holiday Inns) bought the Grenada Royal Hometel chain, one of the very first "suite" hotels in 1984 long before the suites concept was clearly perceived as significant. In 1985 they changed the name to Embassy Suites. To many in the industry, it looked like Holiday was taking a big risk. But now that suite hotels are firmly established in their niche, the Holiday pioneering attitude, which got them in early, has paid off.

IBM pioneered the personal computer. When the decision was made to manufacture them, there was not nearly enough data to prove that it was a wise decision. Yet Frank Carey and John Opel of IBM told their executives that IBM was, indeed, going to become a force in the desktop computer world.

Ford pioneered the Total Quality Management process in the United States for the auto industry. Even though this was late in comparison with the Japanese, Ford still led in the adoption of the process in America.

THE LEVERAGE OF PIONEERING

You may have noticed an implication building over the last two and a half chapters; it is now time to make it explicit:

You don't have to be a paradigm shifter to get all the advantages. Just being a paradigm pioneer is sufficient.

What is the likelihood that you will discover the next paradigm? There are too many people out there trying to solve those problems on the shelf; the law of averages says they will get there before you will.

But, as long as you are listening, and pick up on the new paradigm early enough, you can still have all the fun. Notice the important qualification: as long as you are listening. If you don't know what to listen for, you won't hear early enough to be a pioneer. And that is the constant challenge—to listen outside your field for people who are messing around with your rules.

Can this hypothetical advantage be illustrated? Sadly, for America, it is all too easy.

What nation is the best in the world at discovering new paradigms?

Your answer should be the United States of America. Its track record is unchallengeable: Who invented the videocassette recorder? Who invented the personal computer? Who invented the hard disk drive? Who invented Total Quality Management?

Who invented photocopiers? Who invented stereo? Who invented flat screen technology? Who invented integrated circuits? Who invented ceramic superconductors? Who invented the nonelectronic air bag triggers? To name a few recent inventions.

But what nation is the best in the world at paradigm pioneering? That is, at taking someone else's paradigm shift and driving it around the curve out of A and into B, making it commercial, marketable?

Your answer should be Japan.

The Japanese have harvested paradigm shift ideas from around the world: from VCRs (United States) to electronic watches (Switzerland) to diamond coating (USSR), each of which spawned a revolution in its field.

And look at the results. Time and again, because they have been willing to get in early, do the work to complete the rules of the new paradigm so that it can be effectively utilized, the Japanese have gained world dominance.

Getting in early and staying the course. These two principles violate the mentality of the United States's financial industry, which wants safe, secure, quarterly returns. Theirs is the perfect articulation of the settler's mentality. "Is it safe out there?" they ask. If not, they do not offer their support, and the best ideas developed in the United States are left open for the Japanese to pick off and develop at their leisure.

Not only are the Japanese wonderful paradigm pioneers but they have another advantage as a result of using another invented-in-America idea: Total Quality.

Remember when I said in the foreword of this book that one of the keys to the twenty-first century, a requirement for success, would be excellence as manifested in Total Quality Management? Now it is time to return to the discussion of excellence to show how paradigm pioneering and one of the aspects of TQM give paradigm pioneering an extraordinary advantage.

Part of the Total Quality effort is continuous improvement, or *kaizen* as the Japanese call it. *Kaizen* is all about the ability to make very small improvements in processes and products every day. Every day you are expected to find some way to get just one tenth of 1 percent improvement in what you do or make.

In the old American paradigm of management and product development, this seemed like a waste of time. Americans wanted to hit home runs. Big changes were all that were valued. And yet when you take one tenth of 1 percent daily improvement over a 240-day work year, you find that you have improved by 24 percent!

Now, take *kaizen* and add it to the advantage of early entry that the paradigm pioneer gains. What does it do to the slope of B on the Paradigm Curve? If you think about it for minute, you realize that it steepens the slope! (See Figure 11.) That means, you solve more of the problems of the paradigm quicker.

You can call that progress and it wouldn't be inaccurate, but it's much more than that. It is an enormous competitive advantage over anyone getting into the new paradigm after you. "Is it safe out there?" call the settlers. Now the answer is, "Yes, but there's nothing left for you."

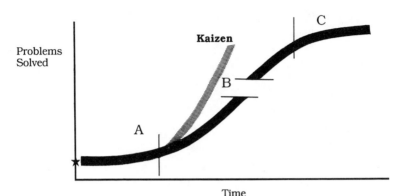

Time

The Result of Continuous Improvement

Figure 11

We have models of this kind of advantage in the real world. We merely have to look to Japan for proof. Take the Walkman, a Sony invention that precipitated a paradigm shift in personal entertainment. Here, by the way, we should acknowledge that Sony not only pioneered the new paradigm but created it as well—ideal behavior.

Sony introduced its Walkman to the U.S. in 1979. It was an innovation heard round the world. Almost immediately, other Japanese companies got into the market. Within three months Panasonic and Aiwa announced their products.

But, just as they were bringing their products out, Sony announced that they had just made their Walkman smaller. It only took a moment for the copycats to realize that Sony had just separated itself from them, so they lowered the prices on their bigger machines and went back to the labs to make smaller ones.

They brought out their smaller models several months later. At which point Sony announced that it had just added FM. To which the copycats responded by lowering the prices of their smaller Walkmans and headed back to their development labs.

Well, more than ten years have passed. Sony has never stopped adding improvements. Look at the list:

auto reverse

bass and treble

special smaller headphones

shock resistance

water resistance

electronic tuning for the radio

smaller still

rechargeable batteries

still smaller

Dolby

an alarm clock

This, of course, doesn't count all the internal manufacturing improvements Sony made that its competitors had to deal with as well.

What's the moral to this little story?

> **Being a paradigm pioneer plus practicing continuous improvement leads to never giving the settlers an even break.**

In the twenty-first century it will be the settlers who are at risk. Reverse engineering will only tell you what the pioneers did in the past. By the time you figure it out, they will be long gone. Every day the settler delays, the more it costs to enter into competition with the pioneers. And less of the market is left for them.

In the twentieth century, giant companies used to wait for the little companies to ''make the market'' and then use their money and reputation to step into the market and take it away.

It won't work that way next time around.

So there is an important trade-off that goes with being a paradigm pioneer: first in—big risk; first in—big potential advantage. That is the trade-off for the paradigm pioneer.

For me, this aspect of the paradigm change is especially interesting because of what it says about the objectivity of science. The most important time for the scientific community, when the pioneers choose the new rules and commit to them, it is an **arational** time (not irrational!). And that time is one of the most important moments of scientific activity.

The message is clear: If you want to be one of the first into the new territory, you cannot wait for large amounts of evidence. In fact, you have to do exactly the opposite. If you want to be early, you must trust your intuition, you must trust your nonrational judgment and take the plunge; make the leap of faith to the new paradigm.

If you wait until the facts are irrefutable, you will be merely a settler and it will probably be too late to gain any special advantage.

"The scales have fallen from my eyes."

CHAPTER 7

What Is the Paradigm Effect?

SO FAR, we understand three principles of the paradigm shift:

1. Paradigms, even as they are successfully solving many problems, always uncover problems that they cannot solve. These problems trigger the search for a new paradigm.

2. Paradigm shifters are almost always outsiders—in that they don't understand the subtleties of the prevailing paradigms and/or have no investment in them.

3. Paradigm pioneers will never have enough proof to make a rational judgment. They will choose to change the paradigm because they trust their intuition.

Now, let us consider the fourth question that was posed in Chapter 3, which, as you recall, focuses on the results of experiencing a paradigm shift. It illuminates the single most important aspect of paradigms and their influence on our ability to discover the future.

How do paradigm shifts affect those who go through them?

Kuhn noticed an unusual kind of commentary that occurred in the writings of scientists who changed their paradigms. Frequently he came across phrases that had a nonscientific flavor to them, a kind of exaggerated description; phrases like, "The scales have fallen from my eyes" (page 122). These expressions indicated that the scientists seemed to be seeing things that they had not seen before.

Why would thoughtful and conscientious scientists use such language? It was not the language of precision or objectivity. A logical explanation would be that the new paradigm **forced them to look in a different direction**. And, since they were looking in a different direction, they had no choice but to see things they had never seen before.

But that is not what Kuhn concluded, because he came across situations in which the scientists were reproducing, as exactly as possible, old experiments—same subjects, same controls, same method of observation—and were still writing about seeing something totally new. The only change in the experiment was the scientists' paradigm.

To quote Kuhn:

> In a sense that I am unable to explicate further, the proponents of competing paradigms practice their trades in different worlds. . . . Practicing in different worlds, the two groups of scientists see different things *when they look from the same point in the same direction.* Again, that is not to say they can see anything they please. Both are looking at the world, and what they look at has not changed. But, in some areas, they see different things, and they see them in different relations one to the other. That is why a law that cannot even be demonstrated to one group of scientists may seem **intuitively** obvious to another (page 150, my emphases).

Put even more strongly: I think what Kuhn is saying is that paradigms act as **physiological filters**—that we quite literally see the world through our paradigms.

Within the paradigm discussion, it means that any data that exists in the real world that **does not fit your paradigm** will have a difficult time getting through your filters. You will see little if any of it. The data that does fit your paradigm, not only makes it through the filter, but is concentrated by the filtering process thus creating an illusion of even greater support for the paradigm.

Therefore what we actually perceive is dramatically determined by our paradigms. What may be perfectly visible, perfectly obvious, to persons with one paradigm, may be, quite literally, invisible to persons with a different paradigm.

This is the **Paradigm Effect.**

The least-worst result of the Paradigm Effect is illustrated when people say, "That's impossible." Those two words can be translated to, "Based on the paradigm we are practicing right now, we don't know how to do it."

The worst-worst result is the physiological effect:

**You are quite literally unable to
to perceive data right before your very eyes.**

But it is not just visual. You listen but you do not hear. You touch but you don't feel. You sniff but you don't smell. All the senses are mediated by the Paradigm Effect.

In 1973, when I came to this point in Kuhn's book, I remember sitting back and understanding a decade's worth of wrong decisions. I had watched people I thought were intelligent make decisions that turned out to be terrible.

For instance, the tremendous resistance by big business to the environmentalists. I had thought the business leaders were just stupid, or arrogant, or too consumed with making money. But most of it, I am now convinced, was a true inability to see what the environmentalists were pointing out. The old paradigms blocked their ability to perceive and understand what was really happening out there in the world.

Today, the vast majority of business people, even those who were part of the initial resistance, would agree that the environment must be protected.

General Motors had the same kind of problem with Ralph Nader. They didn't get what he was trying to tell them. And "not getting it" meant that Nader's consumer-rights position couldn't get through their filters; they were unable to understand.

Remember the father-son battles over length of hair in the 1960s? We laugh at it today, but it was serious business in those days. It was a redefinition of "maleness" and the dads with old rules couldn't handle it.

The same was true of the demographers' response to Paul Ehrlich's plea for Zero Population Growth. A top demographer, Ben Wattenberg, appeared on *Meet the Press* and said things like "The United States will never reduce its birth rate." Because that was the way things were in his paradigm. Today the United States is trending toward ZPG.

And it is not just in business and science, but culture and religion. Time and again we see two religious factions battling over what we on the outside perceive as trivial issues. Yet, if you could step inside the paradigms of those people, you would see looming in front of you a huge issue that is at the core of your belief.

And it is not just something we appreciate in the here and now. How often have we read about experts from the past trying to predict the world we live in today. We find their attempts humorous yet upsetting, given who is speaking:

"The phonograph . . . is not of any commercial value."
—THOMAS EDISON remarking on his own invention to his assistant Sam Insull, 1880

"Flight by machines heavier than air is unpractical and insignificant, if not utterly impossible.—SIMON NEWCOMB, an astronomer of some note, 1902

"Sensible and responsible women do not want to vote."—GROVER CLEVELAND, 1905

"It is an idle dream to imagine that . . . automobiles will take the place of railways in the long distance movement of . . . passengers."—American Road Congress, 1913

"There is no likelihood man can ever tap the power of the atom."—ROBERT MILLIKAN, Nobel Prize winner in physics, 1920

"[Babe] Ruth made a big mistake when he gave up pitching."—TRIS SPEAKER, 1921

"Who the hell wants to hear actors talk?"—HARRY WARNER, Warner Brothers Pictures, 1927

"I think there is a world market for about five computers."—THOMAS J. WATSON, chairman of IBM, 1943

"The odds are now that the United States will not be able to honor the 1970 manned-lunar-landing date set by Mr. Kennedy."—*New Scientist,* April 30, 1964

"There is no reason for any individual to have a computer in their home."—KEN OLSEN, president of Digital Equipment Corporation, 1977

Please notice that the people making these predictions were neither stupid nor trying to mislead. They were, without exception, experts in their field. But, as soon as you understand the Paradigm Effect, you understand that these people just couldn't see past their paradigms.

Tris Speaker, a Hall of Fame batter, focused on Babe Ruth when he was pitching, because that was his frame of reference for the Babe. He had to solve the pitching problems Ruth presented him with in order to be successful; Babe's hitting skills were irrelevant to him. So he ended up thinking it was a mistake to make Ruth a right fielder.

And even Thomas Edison was unable to see the huge potential of his own invention because he did not yet understand the true boundaries and capabilities of the new recording paradigm.

The list goes on and on, and it indicates two things: how powerfully paradigms can trap us into seeing the world in only one way; and how wrong experts can be because of that entrapment.

I now understand that if one is to be able to explore the future well, the most important thing to know is how much influence our paradigms exert on our perception of the world around us.

The Paradigm Effect has been observed in the fields of linguistics, anthropology, cognitive psychology, as well as in many areas of business and education.

The importance of Kuhn's book is that it brings a pivotal group into the discussion; he showed that even scientists are dramatically influenced by their paradigms. They have no special immunity from this kind of influence on their perception!

A paradigm, then, is like a two-edged sword. When swung the "right" way, it cuts the world into discrete bits of refined information that give the paradigm practitioner very subtle vision. That's the good side of the paradigm.

Have you ever been in a situation in which you are explaining something to someone and they say, "How did you see that?" And you answer, "It's obvious." They are amazed at your perception. That's the power of your paradigm letting you see that which is not obvious to people who are unschooled in your paradigm.

A high school friend of mine who is now a radiologist at the Mayo Clinic told me about his training in medical school when he was learning to read X rays. He said that initially he just couldn't see anything that made sense in the negatives. And then one day, "it was all clear. Right there in front of me!" He had learned the "X-ray reading" paradigm.

When the paradigm sword is swung the "wrong" way, it cuts the practitioner away from data that runs counter to the paradigm. At best, the practitioner will write off the data as "impossible" or "inaccurate," and, at worst, will be incapable of perceiving the data at all!

> **So, we see best what we are supposed to see. We see poorly, or not at all, that data that does not fit into our paradigm.**

When that "wrong" data shows up, we will either ignore it as irrelevant or actually distort it until it fits our prevailing paradigm. (Now, go back to page 87 and find the two *to*'s in the boxed section.)

Let me suggest that we can dramatically improve our exploratory skills, by knowing consciously how our present paradigms interfere with our perceptions of the future.

What is defined as "impossible" today is impossible only in the context of present paradigms.

Too often, the future of our business, of our industry, of our nation, exists just outside the boundaries of the prevailing paradigm, impossible to see.

And this is equally true for certain kinds of innovation. When someone offers us a **paradigm-enhancing** innovation—one that improves upon what we are already practicing—we see that easily. But when someone offers us a **paradigm-shifting** innovation, we find ourselves resistant to it, because it just doesn't fit the rules we are so good at.

To improve our ability to anticipate and innovate, we must understand and appreciate the Paradigm Effect. To see the future more clearly, we must put aside the certainties of our present paradigms and begin to examine the fringes for the people who are changing them.

By understanding the Paradigm Effect, we can lift ourselves above its power to blind and begin to search for that which will be our future.

CHAPTER 8

Twenty-two Examples
More or Less

UP TO THIS POINT, I have spent most of your time sharing a generalized picture of how paradigms shift. Now it is time to illustrate with historical examples. From over five hundred examples I have collected over the past two decades, I have picked some I think illustrate the power and range of this idea.

Each example has a special emphasis—the role of the outsider, the inability of the insiders to understand what was going on, the powerful perceptual influence of paradigms, the birth of the new paradigm even as the old is doing well. I will point out these aspects as it is appropriate.

Let us begin with a couple of personal examples that also illustrate the physiological filtering I described in the last chapter. Let me give you two puzzles. Please do them as instructed, if you want to experience the filtering effect.

Below is a column of numbers. They **are** in the base 10. Add them **in your head** as quickly as you feel comfortable. Do not use a pencil. Then write the sum at the bottom of the numbers.

$$1000$$
$$40$$
$$1000$$
$$30$$
$$1000$$
$$20$$
$$1000$$
$$\underline{10}$$

If your total is 5,000, then you are in agreement with 95 percent of the people who add these numbers. In Europe, in Asia, almost everyone makes the same mistake. Add the numbers again, please. If you are still getting 5,000 (like I did three times in a row), then read the next paragraph for the correct answer.

Now, the question is: Why do so many people arrive at 5,000 for their sum? The answer has to do with our confidence in our adding. Most of us add it right to 4,090, and then screw up completely carrying the 1. The correct answer is 4,100.

Remember that one of the rules of paradigms is that the more invested you are in one set of rules, the harder it is to see an alternative? I was at the Deerborn (Michigan) Hyatt hotel in 1984 with a leadership group of the American Institute of Certified Public Accountants. I thought this problem would make an interesting lead off example. So I asked them how good they were at adding and subtracting. They thought that was funny.

Then I gave them the numbers problem, uncovering one line at a time on an overhead projector. When I had shown them all the numbers, I covered them back up and asked for the answer. Without exception, all 280 of them said, "Five thousand!"

I asked them to indicate how sure they were of their answer by raising their hands if they felt confident: **All** the hands went up. Then I uncovered the numbers so they could see them again and, just as I was about to point out their error, someone from the front row said in a low accusing voice, "You changed the slide!"

How could these people, the leaders in their field, make such a stupid mistake? It had to do with how confident they were with numbers. But that set of eight numbers is anomalous: It sets you up to adding wrong, not right. Yet no one in the audience saw the correct answer or at least had the courage to contradict all their fellow "leaders."

This, by the way, is a good example of the power of a group practicing the same paradigm, erring together, and not being able to admit to the error for fear of disagreeing with the majority.

A trivial set of numbers. A nontrivial example of the power of paradigms.

For those of you who would like redemption, here is another "little" puzzle. Figure 12 is a square defined by four dots. A square, by the way, is a rectangle with four equal sides and four 90-degree angles. Please move two of the dots and create a square twice as big as the one defined by the dots as they are presently arranged: Take no more than thirty seconds to solve this. If you cannot, you will find the answer on page 97.

Figure 12

The trick to this problem is the word "square." Most people try to solve it by keeping the sides of the larger square parallel with the smaller one. And, of course, that won't work. But, just as soon as you figure out that a diamond is a square on point, you realize that by connecting one diagonal and then moving the two other dots to make the remainder of the points, you've got a square twice as large as the original one.

I have tested this problem by substituting the word "diamond" for the word "square" in the instructions: "Create a diamond twice as large as the square"—and everyone solves the problem in less than ten seconds. (See Figure 13.)

Here you have your "square" paradigm getting in the way. Can you have a "square" paradigm? Sure. You have rules and regulations that set the boundaries of "squareness" and more rules for solving problems within those boundaries—how to make little squares and big squares, for instance. This set of rules is very small. But you know it. And, hiding in those rules is the "diamond as square" rule, if you remember it. But if you don't,

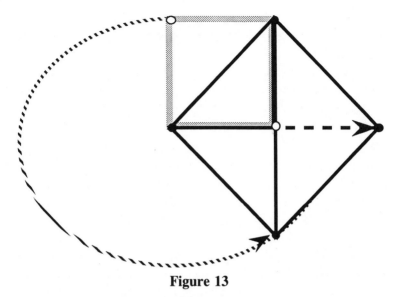

Figure 13

then you can't see past the familiar set of rules to find the other. The word "square" creates a filter that diminishes your capacity to see the right answer.

Let me share another example that is very visceral and gets you in contact with your boundaries almost immediately. In Ellen J. Langer's wonderful book, *Mindfulness,* she offers on page 22 a little test that illustrates a cultural paradigm: Start by moistening your mouth with your saliva. From the back of your teeth to the tip of your tongue, it should be wet, smooth, comfortable. It should feel pleasant because a moist mouth is a natural and healthy condition.

Next, Langer asks you to take a little paper cup or glass and spit some of that saliva into the container. Now, sip it back in.

What is your response? Disgust? That's what it is for most

Westerners. Why? It is your own body fluid. You just had it **in your mouth** two seconds ago. And yet we have cultural rules that we learn when we are very young (spitting is nasty and to be spit upon is an insult and spit is unhealthy) that bound our behaviors and set our actions such that even thinking about sipping our own saliva revolts us. Langer's point is simple and direct. And all about paradigms.

Just a couple more little examples. First, for those who wear glasses: When is the last time you saw your frames or lenses? Upon reflection, most people conclude that it was either the last time they looked in a mirror or in the morning when they put them on. What happens as soon as they are on? The frame data in your field of view disappears, doesn't it? It does for most people. And where does that data go? It is right before your very eyes. And yet, eyeglass wearers have the ability to eliminate it from their consciousness. Why? Because it is not useful. And one of the things our paradigms do is to define what is important and what is not. And then we ignore/eliminate the input of the unnecessary.

Think of all the data around you that you are keeping out: the hum of the hard disk drive, the reflection from a window, the chirp of a bird, the rumble of the train, the movement of the car, the creak of your chair. Because you are reading right now, that other data is not only useless but even dysfunctional unless you can eliminate it. So you do.

How many times have you caught yourself having driven several blocks "on automatic"? How did you do that? It speaks to how effective your driving paradigm is that you can literally disconnect your consciousness from it and still proceed.

Not only do we eliminate unnecessary data. We also have the capacity to alter it to fit our expectations. One of the best examples of doing that is close to one hundred years old.

VISION ASKEW

At the Hanover Institute in Germany in the late nineteenth century, the following experiment was conducted. Subjects were asked to put on goggles that had inverting lenses in them. That is, when the subjects looked through the lenses, the world appeared upside down. The purpose of the research was to see how subjects responded to this unusual situation.

Now, if you or I were asked to speculate on the ways the subjects might respond to this predicament we would probably guess that they would learn to adjust to "upsidedownness." (However, we would also worry about these goggled people trying to walk down steps or negotiate street crossings.)

How did the subjects deal with the upside-down-vision problem? While some took a short time and others took many hours, all who wore the goggles ultimately reported to the experimenters that **the world was back to normal.**

Their solution was simple: Turn the information right side up! Somehow they were able to unconsciously search out the vision-control mechanism inside their brains and "click the switch" that turned the information 180 degrees around! That is an amazing solution to the problem.

To put it into paradigm language, when confronted with the choice of creating new rules to deal with the upside-down information or keeping the old rules and altering the data, the subjects of this experiment did the most efficient thing: They kept their rules and changed the data. And that change allowed them to deal with the world efficiently and effectively at minimum disruption to their way of seeing the world.

This simple experiment is a very powerful demonstration of our ability to manipulate the **physiological** information coming into our minds. Who would have guessed that, by choice, we could so dramatically alter our sensory input? We have far more control over what we perceive and how we perceive than we realize.

We can also create data that does not exist. I have two powerful examples of just that kind of behavior—both driven by personal paradigms.

BUDWEISER BEER CAN'TS

In 1977, in Boca Raton, Florida, I was giving the paradigm lecture to a group of IBM managers. Shortly after I finished, a young man from the audience came up and said, ''I now understand something I could never explain before.'' (Words like that are music to my ears!) This was his story:

At that time he was an avid scuba diver. Quite often he dove to the depths of 100–150 feet to check out fish traps he had off the coast of Miami Beach. Because that area is well trafficked by expensive yachts, lots of garbage is strewn along the ocean floor, especially beer cans. His problem had been caused by the fact that when he saw Budweiser beer cans down at the 150-foot level, he clearly saw their red labels.

Why did that bother him? If you understand the physics of light, you know that the color red cannot penetrate through 150 feet of water. All that you have left at that depth is green and the few other colors far toward the ultraviolet end of the spectrum. There is no color red at that depth! And that is what bothered him. He knew he shouldn't be seeing red.

So, how was he able to see the color that could not be there? He saw the red label because he knew the "correct model" of the Budweiser beer can. That is, he knew the color it was supposed to be, and, in order to make it fit the rules, he literally colored the can in his mind. In reality, that label could not show up as red. But, as far as his perception was concerned, it was Budweiser red.

Since that time, when I've shared his story with some of my audiences, other scuba divers come up to tell me that they see the coloring of fish at depths where their colors shouldn't register. But, because they know the correct coloring of the fish, they see it. One diver said, "When I first see them, usually they don't have much color at all. But, within five to ten seconds, they are as brilliant as I know them to be." Interesting language, "know them to be."

A TASTELESS TALE

For me the beer can example is cute and illustrative. There is another story that is sad and illustrative. In the early 1980s, I was in Colorado speaking on paradigms. It was a before-dinner speech so I stayed to eat. During the meal, the woman sitting next to me told me her paradigm story.

Several years before, she had gone to the doctor about a series of headaches and been diagnosed as having a large brain tumor. They operated. The tumor was benign and they removed it. She recalled waking up the morning after the operation and eating breakfast. While she had no pain, she noticed that her senses were a little "foggy." In particular, the food did not taste as good as it usually did.

When her doctor stopped by to visit her, he asked if she had any questions. She said, "Doctor, how long will it take for the drugs to wear off. Things don't taste quite as good as they did before the operation."

She said he took more than half a minute before he replied, "My dear, you must understand. The part of the brain we had to remove contained all your ability to taste and smell. You can't taste anything."

And he was right. From that moment forward, she hasn't tasted anything. But she **had tasted** her breakfast before he told her.

Where had those flavors come from?

She had reconstructed them using the patterns of taste and smell she knew from the past. She literally created those flavors as she expected them to be even though, physiologically, no data was stimulating her to do that.

In these examples, we see the power of our expectations, which are derived from our paradigms, to generate information that does not exist in the real world. This explains many of the disagreements we see between people of different viewpoints.

Both believe they are right and the other is wrong; the truth may be that both are right according to their paradigms.

Do not underestimate the implications of these examples. They illustrate the physiological power of the rules to quite literally alter information, adding or subtracting to reality, to make it "right."

Let's take a look at how our paradigms of expertise influence the way we perceive the world.

THE CHESS MASTERS

In 1973, Herbert Simon, Nobel Prize winner in economics from Carnegie-Mellon University, was studying perception in chess players with fellow professor of psychology William C. Chase. Their study demonstrates the influence of paradigms. The essence of the research is as follows.

Chase and Simon enlisted three chess players with international rankings, three intermediate chess players, and three who were novice players to be their subjects.

Behind a movable partition, the experimenters set up a partially played chess game. Then, for each subject, the partition was removed and the subject was given five seconds to look at the board. After five seconds, the partition was replaced and the subject was asked to re-create on a blank chessboard as accurately as possible what he had seen during the five seconds.

The contrast between the master chess players and novices was the most dramatic. As you might guess, the masters did very well, indeed. Their average accuracy, with twenty chess pieces on the board, was 81 percent! That is very impressive recall with just five seconds of observation.

The novice chess players' performances were poor—about 33 percent of the pieces were correctly recalled.

Clearly the difference between the two groups was significant.

Now, if you were to stop the experiment at this point and speculate on the difference, you might come up with several theories.

1. The master players have amazing memories.

2. Playing the game well makes you better at remembering piece location.

3. The masters have special tricks for recalling the pieces.

Chase and Simon then proceeded with the second part of the experiment. This time, they altered one factor: The chess pieces were arranged randomly by computer with no attention paid to the rules of the game. Again, the three different groups of players were given the same amount of time to look at the new setup. And, again, they were asked to re-create what they saw on empty chessboards.

What happened this time? Surprisingly, the championship chess players' performances collapsed. Their placement accuracy plummeted. To be exact, their placement was reduced to a percentage worse than the beginners'!

What happened has to do with paradigms. The chess paradigm was removed, and, as a result, the subtle and accurate perception of the master chess players, created by long hours of practice and play, was rendered useless. With the rules, they could draw inferences of location and relationship that gave them incredible accuracy. But, once those rules were gone, their subtle vision was eliminated. Their paradigm gave them wonderful vision within the boundaries of the game. When the paradigm was removed, the masters were masters no longer.

All over the world, we have seen experts who were trapped by the same phenomenon: Within their boundaries, they are brilliant; when the rules change, they are helpless.

Mark Twain shows us the positive side of this perception-shaping by our paradigms.

THE RIVERBOAT PILOT

Some years ago, I was watching a dramatization of *Life on the Mississippi* by Samuel Clemens (Mark Twain) on the Public Broadcasting System. One scene made me sit up and watch intently, because the discussion was a beautiful articulation of the influence of paradigms.

The novice riverboat pilot and his friend were watching the sunset, and the friend was waxing poetic about the beauty of the river. But, where the friend saw loveliness, the pilot-in-training saw something very different. After the segment concluded, I went immediately to my library and found the book. It took me fifteen minutes of searching to find the passage from which the scene was created. Let me share it with you as Twain wrote it:

First, the poetry:

A broad expanse of the river was turning to blood; in the middle distance the red hue brightened into gold, through which a solitary log came floating, black and conspicuous; in one place a long, slanting mark lay sparkling upon the water; in another the surface was broken by boiling, tumbling rings, that were as many-tinted as an opal; where the ruddy flush was faintest, was a smooth spot that was covered with graceful circles and radiating lines, ever so delicately traced.

Twain concludes:

I stood like one bewitched. I drank it in, in a speechless rapture. The world was new to me, and I had never seen anything like this at home.

But, as he traveled the river learning to pilot, Twain's perception was changed by his education and he reflected on how he would view the same scene from his pilot's point of view:

If that sunset scene had been repeated, I should have looked upon it without rapture, and should have commented upon it, inwardly after this fashion: This sun means that we are going to have wind tomorrow; that floating log means that the river is rising, small thanks to it; that slanting mark on the water refers to a blue reef which is going to kill somebody's steamboat one of these nights, if it keeps on stretching out like that; those tumbling "boils" show a dissolving bar and a changing channel there; the lines and circles in the

slick water over yonder are a warning that that troublesome place is shoaling up dangerously.

His conclusion to this change of vision reflects the dilemma
of any expert:

> All the value of any feature of it [the river] had for me
> now was the amount of usefulness it could furnish
> toward compassing the safe piloting of a steamboat.

As Kuhn noted, and I am trying to reinforce, when you
change your paradigm, or, in the case of Mark Twain, when you
learn a paradigm, the world quite literally is seen anew.

What Mark Twain illustrates perfectly with this story is the
coming of vision that accompanies the learning of a new paradigm. You and I would look at the river and never see it the way
he did as a riverboat pilot . . . until we took the training ourselves.

DINOSAUR DEATHS

In science, as Thomas Kuhn well illustrated, we see the
paradigm-shift rules play themselves out continually. If you have
been following the revolution in dinosaur extinction theory, then
you know that it was **not** a paleontologist who came up with the
meteorite-impact theory of catastrophic extinction, but a Nobel-
prize–winning physicist, Luis Alvarez, who saw a funny layer of
iridium in soil samples from the same epoch as that of the dinosaur disappearance.

Read the scientific literature and you will find the same kind of questioning of his credibility—what is a physicist doing in our field!—followed by the acts of faith of some of the paleontologists, including the brilliant Stephen Jay Gould, who began to examine the evidence.

Now it is almost a foregone conclusion that it was a meteorite strike. The big questions are: Where did it hit? Was it just one? Did it cause volcanic activity that added to the damage? Did it superheat the air as it ripped through the atmospheric envelope of the planet and cook the dinosaurs like meat on a spit? Did the impact cause a "nuclear winter" and darken the planet for months or years?

These questions, which are now the problems to be solved with the new paradigm, could not have been generated with the old paradigm of gradual extinction.

SUPERCONDUCTORS

The discovery of "warm" superconductors was made by a Swiss physicist, Alex Mueller, who is an IBM fellow at its laboratory in Zurich. He follows the older, other-field model of paradigm shifter just like Alvarez. Dr. Mueller was assisted by a young physicist, George Bednorz, who hadn't established his reputation yet. In fact, it was an error by this young man—not setting the oven hot enough—that accidentally provided the first samples of the ceramic compound. Had he been more experienced, he probably wouldn't have made the error.

I hope you noticed it was a **ceramic** material that became superconducting under much warmer conditions than any other material ever tested. Yet, anyone who knows anything about electricity knows that ceramics are used to insulate from not to conduct electricity. Dr. Mueller, who didn't know the superconducting paradigm, had this feeling about ceramics. And his intuition proved to be Nobel Prize-winningly correct.

STAYING AFTER SCHOOL

This pattern of not knowing any better happens in business all the time. I was lecturing to a group of salespeople for Josten's, a Minnesota company that sells recognition products to schools and businesses. They produce class rings, school yearbooks, recognition awards, among other things. Afterward, a man of Hispanic background came up to chat. He told me that he had shifted a paradigm. "I was taking over for my father who had been the salesperson for Josten's in Puerto Rico." He said that his father had prepared him to go out for the first time to meet the school principals who were his customers.

"The schedule he gave me was to take me all week to complete," he explained. "The first day, I was running late, so by the time I got to the school I was supposed to visit, the principal had gone home."

He didn't want to get behind schedule so he asked the school secretary for the address of the principal and then went to his house to visit him. He made the sale.

With that success in mind, the next two days he worked on into the evening by going to see principals in their homes.

He arrived back at the office two days early. "My father was very upset with me for not having finished my schedule," he told me. "So I explained that I had seen everyone and was successful with almost all of them."

"That's impossible," his father said. Then the son explained what he had done—visiting the principals in their homes. "My father, he couldn't believe that I would do such a thing. We were always supposed to visit principals in their schools."

But what the son had discovered was that away from the school, where the principals weren't so harried by the pressures of the day, he got to talk to them uninterrupted. It was an easier sell.

His discovery made him one of the top salespeople for Josten's and others emulated him and his technique.

Here is the young outsider not knowing he wasn't supposed to visit principals in their homes. To fulfill the obligations of his schedule, he did. And changed, fundamentally, the definition of when and where was the best time to do the selling.

HOUSE-TO-HOUSE SELLING

I was given another sales story from an Arthur Andersen accountant; also a young person. He was asked to work with a privately held Canadian construction company. At a strategy meeting he attended to get acquainted, he was listening to the planning discussion when he heard something that made him curious—the plan to build new model homes.

In his innocence, he asked what the model homes were used for. The answer: to show to customers when they came looking for a new home. "Our salespeople are there."

Now the accountant was even more curious: "What do you mean the salespeople are there? All the other companies I work with have the salespeople go out to the customer. They don't wait for the customer to come to them."

One of the company VPs patiently explained, "Well, that's not possible in our business. That's just the way it is. Anyway, how would you find our customer?"

The accountant told me he thought about that question for a couple of minutes and then interjected himself into the discussion again. "Well, if it was me I'd have them find houses with For Sale signs in front and go up to talk to the owners. They're your potential customers."

At first, the accountant said, they started to tell him to be quiet. But then, the patriarch of the group began to play with the idea. "I suppose we could hire a salesperson to do that sort of thing. It wouldn't cost that much."

So they tried this new accountant's silly idea. You can guess the rest. It has worked amazingly well. Of course, it breaks all the rules. And, of course, it has opened up whole new territories for this company, because they have found that while they are trying to sell new homes, they inadvertently stumbled into the opportunity of reselling older homes, bought from the people buying their new homes. They use their construction crews to fix them up, clean them up, make them a better buy on the used house market, and add them to the inventory book their sales-people carry.

Who would have thought that door-to-door house selling could possibly work? That's the way it is with paradigm shifts.

MEASURING RIGHT, MEASURING WRONG

Sony Corporation gave me a wonderful example of how seemingly little aspects of a paradigm can block the single insight needed to complete a breakthrough. This one has to do with compact disc players.

As anyone who has followed this technology knows, Sony was one of the first into the fray. Their first portable CD player was hailed for its technological prowess. One hi-fi magazine called it "second generation technology the first time around."

Why was Sony the leader? The obvious answer comes from examining when they started their research of laser music discs: the early 1970s.

It sounds great until you also learn that around 1976 they stopped their research, concluding that laser discs were not appropriate for music. Curious, don't you think?

It wasn't until 1979 that they were induced back into the audio laser disc business by Phillips of the Netherlands. Phillips called Sony to talk about establishing a world standard for audio CDs, because it knew that Sony had done extensive work in the area.

Typical of the Japanese, Sony didn't say, "That's a stupid idea because we've already checked it out." Instead they invited Phillips to come to Japan to talk about it.

Phillips sent a small team. Again, typical of the Japanese, Sony assembled the team who had done the research. And, again typically, they let the Phillips people make their presentation first.

As the story goes, the Phillips researcher started with a disclaimer stating that they knew Sony was way ahead of them, so whatever Sony wanted to do was fine. Then he proceeded to show them the prototype of the laser music disc they were working on—about one-half inch larger in diameter than today's disc.

"We think this is about the right size," he said.

Now I can't be positive what the Japanese thought as they saw that little disc, but I'm willing to speculate. I'll bet it was the Japanese equivalent of "Oh, shit!"

Because guess what size disc the Japanese had been working on the entire time? Remember the old paradigm? LPs—twelve inches in diameter! That was their model. And if a disc one-third that size could hold more than an hour's worth of music, what do you think a twelve-inch disc could hold? About eighteen hours of music!

And the Japanese looked at that eighteen hours of capacity and asked themselves two very intelligent questions. How would we program the eighteen hours? One hour of Sinatra plus one hour of Beethoven plus one hour of the Beatles plus . . . well, you get the idea. The second question they asked was: How do you price it—$199.95?

Those are both important questions, if you have accepted the size as a certainty. And they had.

No one, at least no one with any authority, ever asked the question: What is the right size for a laser music record?

And here we see paradigms getting in the way of innovation. The Japanese were trapped by a boundary, in this case, the boundary measured **in space** rather than **in time**. So twelve inches became a limiting factor. It was perfectly easy to calculate how big the CD needed to be if you asked what was the appropriate amount of time capacity for a record.

And that is exactly what the Phillips people had done. Two Phillips engineers gave me the rest of the story. They said that the director of research and development for Phillips was having supper with the famous Berlin Philharmonic conductor, Herbert von Karajan. The director asked the conductor what he thought was the proper length of a record. Karajan answered, "If you can't get Beethoven's Ninth on one side, it is not long enough."

I find it interesting that Beethoven, 150 years after his death, set the time standard for one of the most advanced music playback technologies of the twentieth century.

But let us not miss the moral of the story: Sony, known for its wonderful innovation and engineering, had been stopped by part of a paradigm, the boundary rules. They were unable to look beyond the twelve-inch LP to see their future.

A STEAL OF A STEEL

Making a profit from recycled steel is impossible. That's what the president of Nucor Corp., pioneer in steel mini-mills, was told when he went, as an entrepreneur, to talk to a major steel company. Kenneth Iverson, Nucor's chairman, had this idea: Why not use the scrap steel we have all over the United States and make "recycled" steel from it with electric arc furnaces, nonunion workers paid very well, and in small regional plants instead of giant national ones. It had already been tried in Canada by an inventor/entrepreneur named Jerry Heffernan in the early 1960s, but if you were in the steel industry, you knew that Iverson would never see a profit.

Twenty years later Nucor and other minimill companies such as North Star Steel Minnesota make close to a 20-percent return on investment and have taken away market after market from the big integrated steelmakers. First it was just steel re-bar for roadways. That had transportational advantages—regional plants were close to where the roads were being built. Then it was steel pipe. And then, in 1989, Nucor announced it would begin shipping flat-rolled sheet steel, which had always been considered untouchable by the big guys.

"The technology revolution is going to be very threatening to established producers," said Peter Marcus, a steel industry analyst for Paine Webber, in an October 17, 1989, article in *The Wall Street Journal*. He added that the old steel companies have "got too much invested in the old stuff and they can't get their workers to be flexible."

What was considered impossible in steel production is now a reality. And that's the way it is so often with new paradigms. Those old-paradigm impossibilities are fully within the capabilities of the new ones.

For Sony an entire market was blocked by one little rule. And the minimill companies are rewriting the entire steel industry paradigm. Both created huge opportunities for the pioneering organization and put the practitioners of the old paradigm at grave risk.

BAGGING IT

I was flipping through a *Popular Science* magazine back in 1984 when I came upon a little article about a new approach to air bags for cars. The company identified in the article was Breed Corporation of Lincoln Park, New Jersey. They had devised an air bag trigger that, air bag included, costs about fifty dollars.

Articles like that always stop me. I knew that GM and Ford and Chrysler had always talked about the cost of air bags as, at a minimum, between $500 and $600. What was going on here?

It turns out to be a wonderful paradigm story. First, we need to understand what Breed is good at—making explosive devices, such as detonators for hand grenades.

Then we have to understand that the president of Breed somehow saw a connection between what he did and air bags. The story goes that he was reading about air bags and ran into two phrases that captured his attention: "Air bags **go off on impact**." (He knew how to do that.) And, "Air bags **blow up**," which he knew how to do, too. So he called in a couple of his engineers and told them to see if they could apply Breed technology to the air-bag problem.

Less than a year later and with less than $400,000 spent in R and D, Breed had developed a trigger for the air bag. And it is the trigger, not the bag, that is the expensive part.

Figure 14 is a schematic. I'll talk you through it. The ball bearing (A) sits in a larger chamber (the white area) (B); it would like to roll around in there but it can't because it is pinned up against the back wall by the lever (C). You can see where the

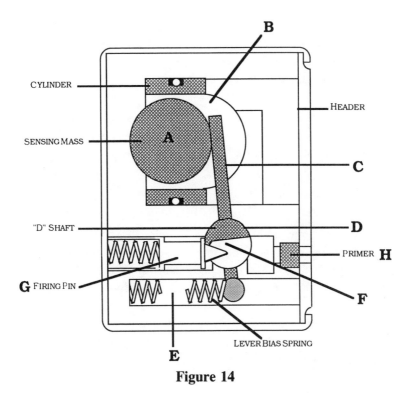

B

CYLINDER

HEADER

SENSING MASS

A

C

"D" SHAFT

D

PRIMER **H**

G FIRING PIN

F

LEVER BIAS SPRING

E

Figure 14

lever rotates (D) and at the other end of the lever a spring (E) pushes against it, creating the pressure to hold the ball bearing in place.

Now, when you hit something, what does the ball bearing want to do? Go forward, right? But it can't because of the pressure of the lever. At least it can't until it gains enough momentum, which occurs when you hit something solid at nine miles per hour or faster, generating about four g's of force. Then the ball pushes forward, straightening up the lever, rotating its axis, lifting the little flange (F) that holds the firing pin in place. With the pin released, the spring behind it drives the pin (G) across the gap to stab the primer (H). The primer explodes and the force of the explosion squeezes together two chemicals that, when brought together in this way, create a gas that expands and inflates the air bag.

All this happens in one thirtieth of a second and instead of you kissing your steering wheel (which happens even if you are wearing your shoulder belt), you kiss an air bag.

This is done for fifty bucks a pop.

Sounds great, right? Elegant. Simple. Inexpensive. What a deal! So the Breed folks went to visit General Motors. And what do you think GM said? They told them to take a hike. In the summer of 1990, I spoke to the Cadillac division of GM. I mentioned this example. Afterward, two engineers came up to me, chagrined. They said, "We interviewed those guys. And, you are right, we didn't give them the time of day." Then they said maybe they should talk to them again.

All the American car companies turned them down. We can forgive Lee Iacocca at Chrysler because he had already committed to the product they would install in all their American-built cars starting in the fall of 1989. So, Lee was being a paradigm pioneer. Thank you, Mr. Iacocca.

When I talked to the people at Breed in late 1990, they told me that two car companies in the world were testing their system: Jaguar and (here we go again) Toyota. Toyota is testing in Japan because they fear the threat of civil litigation if it malfunctions in lawsuit-crazy America. But, if it needs to be perfected, you can count on Toyota to do exactly that.

And look at the advantage they will have in costs over the American electronic version: $600 a pop for the United States system; $50 a pop for the Breed system used by the Japanese. Do you think the American car companies will cry unfair competition again?

Before we leave this example, let me take some of the heat off GM and Ford. Think about it: In walks the representative from Breed who basically starts his pitch by saying, in effect, "Hi, I'm from a hand-grenade company and I'm here to help you."

What's the logical response to that statement? Or try out this one: "In the last year two of our engineers with less than half a million dollars in expenses solved the problem that your entire industry over the last twenty years has been unable to solve with more than one billion dollars in expenses." What's the logical response to that?

We can understand, within the context of the Paradigm Effect, why it was so hard for the automakers to get serious about Breed's claims. They were **really** outsiders. Every number they presented violated good sense and years of research information.

Why waste time checking it out?

For you and me there is another message from this example: You and I would have had just as tough a time if Breed had showed up on our doorsteps with solutions to our impossible problems. We have to be ready to listen to the Breeds of the world if we want early access to the paradigm shifts that will change our world.

NEW PHOTOGRAPHY

This story is something of a myth in corporate circles because so many companies missed a major opportunity.

In the late 1940s, a man walked into one of the laboratories of a major photography company to demonstrate his concept of a new kind of photography. He brought along a bright red box that had inside it a shiny steel plate, a secret charging device, and a light bulb. He also brought, in a separate container, some fine black powder.

In front of a company researcher, he carefully went through his process, step by step. By the end of his demonstration, he had created, using only his unusual equipment, a faint but perceptible photograph.

Now, the inventor never recorded what was said to him as he finished. But the comments probably focused on his having no developer, no fix, no film, and no darkroom! And probably a concluding comment such as, "Why would we possibly be interested in such an invention. It is not really even photography!"

Whatever was said, the company's action was clear: He was treated the way most paradigm shifters are; he was shown to the door. Thanks, but no thanks. Not only did that company reject his idea but so did forty-two others.

Ultimately, the inventor, Chester Carlson, had the last laugh. With the help of the Battelle Corporation, he improved his invention and found a company, the Halloid Corporation, that was willing to develop his photographic process, which we now call xerography. What Chester Carlson invented was a set of rules and regulations for electrostatic photography. Only Halloid, which ultimately changed its name to Xerox Corporation, had the foresight to see that this new paradigm was worthy of commercial development. I am sure IBM and Kodak and 3M and all the other companies that turned down Chester Carlson would love to have a second chance.

THE HUMAN-POWERED AIRPLANE

The name Dr. Paul D. MacCready will go down in the history books of aviation for an unusual but wonderful reason. He was the inventor of the first successful human-powered plane. And the paradigm effect was key to his success and others' failures.

It all started with the creation of the Kremer Prize, created by English industrialist Henry Kremer in 1959. This prize, originated in England in 1969 and worth fifty thousand pounds sterling, was offered to the developers of the first human-powered airplane able to fly a prescribed figure-eight course with two turning points not less than one-half mile apart while negotiating a ten-foot-high marker at the starting line and the finish line of the course.

Colleges and universities around the world competed for this prize. Many engineers considered the task impossible. But Mac-Cready put an end to that opinion on August 23, 1977, when his plane, *The Gossamer Condor*, pedal-powered and piloted by Bryan Allen, flew the course according to the rules.

Kremer immediately created a second competition, this time to fly across the English Channel with human power. Within two years, in response to the prize of one hundred thousand pounds sterling, MacCready's team did it again, with *The Gossamer Albatross*.

So, what has this to do with paradigms? In a short article written for *Science Digest*, in March 1983, MacCready explained why it was he and not the specialists in aeronautical engineering who won the prize:

"My secret weapon was a complete lack of experience in aircraft-wing structural design while, at the same time, having a familiarity with hang gliders and fragile model airplanes. Our competitors also knew about hang gliders, but they were thwarted by knowing so much about standard techniques."

MacCready suggests that his human-powered plane experience made him begin noticing how often people were stopped from doing things by "barriers that really didn't exist." He writes:

"I soon found that a dominant factor in the way our minds work is the buildup of patterns [paradigms] that enable us to simplify the assimilation of complex inputs. But this same patterning can be a weakness as well as a strength. The patterning makes it hard for a new idea to get fair treatment."

Because Paul MacCready had a different set of rules than his competitors who were rigorously trained in the field, he was able to solve the problem with his alternative paradigm.

CHERNOBYL BLINDNESS

I was giving a lecture to a power utility that has nuclear plants. After I finished, David M. Valeri, one of their nuclear training instructors, came up to me and asked me if I knew about what had happened at Chernobyl.

I said I was aware, as most people were, of the meltdown and the release of radioactivity, but that was all. He said that there was another part of the story that very few people knew about, that it was tragic, and that it illustrated perfectly the kind of paradigm blindness I had just talked about.

He sent me a paper entitled "Chernobyl Notebook," written in June 1989 by G. Medvedev—one of the Soviet scientists who was involved in the post-accident cleanup. The document was an attempt to re-create in a narrative, as accurately as possible, what happened at Chernobyl. Mr. Valeri told me to check page 28. At that point, the narrative describes behavior by the nuclear engineers at the plant shortly after the explosion.

The engineers were trying to figure out what happened. The one thing they "knew for sure" was that the reactor was still intact. Why? Because, from their understanding of the design, they knew it just couldn't have blown up.

So they looked outside to see what had happened. All over the ground was the black of graphite right out of the core— massively, fatally radioactive. "Something was scattered around the unit on the asphalt. Very thickly. Something black. . . . But he [Dyatlov, one of the engineers] could not take it in that this was graphite from the reactor. Just as in the turbine room [where Dyatlov had just looked]. There, as well, his eyes had seen the glowing chunks of graphite and fuel. **But his mind would not accept the horrible implication of what he had seen**" (page 29, my emphasis).

These intelligent, well-trained engineers looked right at the proof of reactor explosion, and decided that there was nothing that indicated an explosion. As far as they were concerned the reactor was still intact. And based on that belief, the crew chief

Akomov kept telling people, the press included, that the reactor core was okay.

The evidence was literally right before their eyes. And yet, because of the deep trust they had in their design, they refused to accept the data for what it was.

They died of massive radioactive exposure. But what really killed them was their inability to see past their paradigms.

I want to conclude this chapter with one more example because it is so simple and so powerful. I learned of it on a drive from Denver to Santa Fe. My wife Susan often reads to me when we travel, because I can't read in a car and she doesn't like to drive. It's a good trade-off. She was reading to me from a book entitled *Women's Reality*, by Ann Wilson Schaef. The entire book turned out to be about cultural, gender-related paradigms. For a white male, it is a disturbing and powerful book because it helps us see the world in a fundamentally different way.

One of the stories in the book told of how the author would run a little experiment when she was talking to corporate audiences that were mixed—including white men, women, and minorities. She would ask the audience to do a simple task: "Please list," she would request, "the rules needed to be successful in a white male society?"

Immediately the women and the minorities would begin to write down all the things they knew they had to do to "fit in." Meanwhile, the white males in the audience just sat there, doing nothing, looking around at the women and the minorities writing for all they were worth. After about two minutes, the author said, the discomfort of the white males began to rise to such a level that sometimes she would have to stop the exercise just to keep them from panicking.

Paradigms are like water to fish. They are invisible in many situations because it is "just the way we do things." Often they operate at an unconscious level. Yet they determine, to a large extent, our behavior. As a white male, I cannot write down all those rules. My wife can. My minority friends can.

I hope from these examples the message about paradigms is clear: They have a profound effect on how we live our lives, how we value those things in our lives, how we solve the problems in our lives. They are at the core of who we are and where we are going.

To ignore the power of paradigms to influence your judgment is to put yourself at significant risk when exploring the future.

To be able to shape your future, you have to be ready and able to change your paradigms.

Without caring there can be no quality.

CHAPTER 9

The Most Important Paradigm Shift of the Twentieth Century

HOW COULD IT BE POSSIBLE to identify the "most important" paradigm shift in the twentieth century.

I have been examining these phenomena for almost twenty years and my chief criterion for importance is a paradigm's ability to solve important problems. Based on that standard, I think there is a clear winner. Ironically, we will not reap all its benefits until the second decade of the twenty-first century. But already it has demonstrated its power to transform companies and communities, economies and technologies.

That is why I take the time to point it out now, because I believe it is well on its way and will not be stopped.

To illustrate how powerful this new paradigm is, let me have you respond to a question. In 1962, what were the kinds of judgmental or qualitative terms that you would have used to describe any product with the following three words stamped on it?

Made in Japan

Please list your terms below.

1.

2.

3.

4.

5.

Now compare your list with the one I had been collecting for several years:

Junk	Crummy
Trivial	Second choice
Cheap	Worst choice!
Poor quality	Poor
Unreliable	Copy
Low-tech	Third choice
Tin cans	Imitation
Tacky	Toys
Second rate	Unimportant
Shoddy	Lousy

You get the idea. Now, let's ask another question. Please fill out in the space provided below the descriptive words that you would have used in connection with these three words today:

Made in Japan

1.

2.

3.

4.

5.

Now, let's compare your list with the one I've been collecting:

High-quality	Inexpensive
State of the art	World leader
Highly reliable	Copy
Best in the world	First choice
Fine quality	Sophisticated
First rate	Innovative
Excellent	Best buy
Zero defects	High-tech

As you'll notice, the two lists are filled with antonyms. Because of that, we need to examine what happened in Japan after 1960 to create such a dramatic turn of events? Of course, many of you know the answer, but I want to put it into my context.

They changed their manufacturing paradigm. It actually began in the early 1950s when W. Edwards Deming, an American, was invited by General Douglas MacArthur to come to Japan to present his ideas on high-quality mass production. He so influenced the Japanese that they ultimately created a prize called the Deming Award. It is the most honored of all industrial awards in Japan.

Deming gave them a powerful quality-control and continuous-improvement paradigm. The Japanese then blended in the work of Professor Kaoru Ishikawa of Tokyo University to create the quality-circle paradigm. On top of that, there were other management innovations and cultural traditions already in place that allowed the Japanese to begin to build a new way of management and manufacturing.

So, by the late 1960s and early 1970s, products from Japan began to appear in American stores and automobile showrooms that were impressive in their quality and durability.

American management responded to these anomalies by finding logical explanations, the classic response from the prevailing paradigm community.

Initially, American manufacturers explained it this way: "Well, they have new factories, we have old factories, so, of course, their products should be better than ours. If we had new factories, we could do just as well."

That seemed a good explanation until a series of studies were made comparing the products coming out of factories of equal ages. Then, surprise! Even with same-age factories, the Japanese products were better.

So American management offered a second explanation. "It's Japanese culture. They have a homogeneous culture; their workers are well educated; they speak the same language; they have the same values; they have corporate unions; and, most of their workers are from the rural areas. So, of course, they would be able to produce better products because the communications and agreement would be so much easier than in America where we have a heterogeneous population with multiple languages, sophisticated union leaders, and a whole range of educational backgrounds."

The explanation was generally accepted until the mid-1970s when Sony Corporation built a TV factory in San Diego, California, one of the most heterogeneous of all cities in America—Anglos, blacks, Hispanics; multiple languages, including "Californian." Yet, despite all this diversity, within three years, Sony named the San Diego plant as one of their top ten plants in the world. All of a sudden, American management was left with no explanations, except one: The Japanese management system was superior to ours. They were producing high-quality products not because of a factory advantage or a cultural advantage but because of a management advantage. And, since 1977, when American business finally understood what was going on, we have been running at a frenzied pace to catch up to the Japanese by attempting to learn and implement their management techniques.

Let's take a closer look at some of the basic changes in the rules that have allowed the Japanese to do so well.

David Garwood, a consultant in Total Quality manufacturing has written a book with Michael Bane entitled *Shifting Paradigms: Reshaping the Future of Industry*. Published in

1990, it is one of the finest explanations of the profound changes that are going on in manufacturing driven by the Total Quality process.

Garwood and Bane assembled two lists, one with the old rules of manufacturing and one with the new rules of manufacturing (pages 80–82). Let me share those with you so that you can see how dramatic the change is. Look for the boundary-change rules; look for the redefinition of success. The authors are correct when they say manufacturing is going through a paradigm shift.

The old rules of manufacturing include the following:

1. Bigger is better. As long as you're running a thousand, why not run three thousand. After all, they're practically free, aren't they?

2. Long setup or changeover times are a given; it really doesn't matter since we're amortizing those costs over a large number of units.

3. Lay out the factory by function. Put all the lathes in one place, all the blenders in another. Let the material travel around, sometimes for miles, to the department specializing in turning, blending or whatever, to get the optimum run.

4. More lead time is better. If we order materials earlier, we might get them on time.

5. The measure of productivity is noise and sweat. Keep all the equipment running and people busy all the time.

6. Stick to a rigid chain of command. The further down the chain you go, the less need there is to think.

7. Supervisors' roles are to think and keep people busy; workers' roles are to keep busy and not to think.

8. Do capacity planning by visible backlog. If the stack of materials around the equipment is growing, we need more capacity. If the pile is going down, slow down.

"The old paradigm," Garwood and Bane write, "is built on the slippery slopes of efficiency."

Now here is their new paradigm of manufacturing:

1. Make only as much as you need, not as much as you can.

2. Economic lot size is what is required by the customer, one or one thousand.

3. Eliminate steps and move to a more process flow.

4. Measure productivity by total hours and total cost incurred, not efficiency or utilization.

5. Lead times are short.

6. Brains are best on the line; supervisors must tap all that intelligence so that together the workers and the supervisors can solve the problems.

7. Schedules have credibility, and production fits the schedule.

8. Capacity requirements are visible.

9. Quality, flexibility, and being on time are the meaningful measurements of performance.

According to Garwood and Bane: "We've moved from a capacity-driven to a customer-driven environment."

What Garwood and Bane are trying to tell manufacturers is that it is a new world out there. The game has changed and almost everything about it is substantially different from the old game.

And it is not just manufacturers, but service companies like Marriott Corporation and Federal Express and Cadillac dealerships that are using this new paradigm of quality to provide unprecedented, do-it-right-the-first-time service.

Erie, Pennsylvania, as a community, has set a goal to become a Total Quality community by 1999.

The state of South Carolina has set an equivalent goal.

Mt. Edgecumbe High School in Sitka, Alaska, is applying this paradigm with startling results.

But there is more to this Total Quality movement than just increases in productivity. Let me list for you four more advantages of the TQ paradigm shift that have profound influence on all aspects of our world.

INCREASED INNOVATION

Part of the Total Quality package is asking people to do it better tomorrow than they did today. It's called "continuous improvement" or *kaizen* in Japanese. This starts with a belief that everyone can be inventive and innovative.

I was walking through a corporate headquarters with the CEO of a company that practices Total Quality. He was taking me to the lecture hall where I was to speak to some of his managers. On the way we met a young secretary. The CEO said hello, asked her name, and then asked her, "What have you done today to improve your work, Sarah?" She answered without a moment's hesitation.

I was impressed.

We walked on a little farther. The CEO stopped a young man. Same ritual. The young man had an answer. I was impressed again.

When we got to the lecture hall, the CEO told the stories of those two people to the managers assembled, in a way that honored and celebrated his employees.

Later on, as I reflected on this experience, I realized that this CEO had a reputation for **never** being in his office. He was a classic wanderer. I put two and two together and thought about it in this way: You work in his company; you know you may bump into him anytime; you know exactly what he is going to ask you; so you are always thinking about ways to improve your job. Obviously, it works.

Ayn Rand said it this way in her book *Atlas Shrugged*: "All work is creative work if done by a thinking mind, and no work is creative if done by a blank who repeats in uncritical stupor a routine he has learned from others" (page 946).

Total Quality creates an attitude of constant innovation.

SELF-MANAGEMENT

With increased productivity and innovation comes a growing self-esteem in the workers. This heightened self-respect often leads to the request to self-manage. Workers realize that they can be in charge of themselves far more effectively than a manager can.

The end result is a flattening of the organization and the disappearance of the classic middle manager. That leads to middle management resistance to this paradigm. Logical. But, in the long term, useless. Self-management is the most democratic, most efficient, and most powerful way to get things done. And it frees up those who are middle managers to use their intelligence for more productive and innovative purposes. No more pushing papers, protecting turf, building empires.

THE RETURN OF ARTISTRY AND CRAFTSMANSHIP

Robert Pirsig, in his book *Zen and the Art of Motorcycle Maintenance,* pointed out that the Greeks did not separate art from technology. Both were united, in the Greek culture, by the common bond of quality.

"The root word of technology, *techne,* originally meant 'art.' The ancient Greeks never separated art from manufacture in their minds, and so never developed separate words for them" (page 283).

Artists and craftspeople care deeply for their work. They would never let something mediocre represent them.

Yet in the early twentieth century, efficiency expert Frederick Taylor created a set of rules that fundamentally compromised the craft standards even as it laid the foundation for mass production. Among his rules were these: that everyone should use the same tools; that once the "right" way had been figured out, no one changed it; that the simpler the steps in the assembly process, the better the product; that workers worked and managers solved problems.

The direction of all the Taylor dicta led remorselessly toward mediocrity. Workers were no longer allowed to do the best that they could do, only what they were told to do.

The beauty of the Total Quality movement is that workers are now motivated by their own values to do the best that they can do. That the workers now have permission to improve the products or services allows them to really care about what they are doing.

Without caring there can be no quality.

And with caring, the concept of work changes fundamentally. Caring is reflected directly in your day-to-day behavior. And from that caring comes great enthusiasm and commitment, which leads in a wonderful feedback loop to even greater productivity, innovation, and self-initiation. All of this leads to perhaps the most important advantages.

THE RETURN OF SPIRIT TO THE WORKPLACE

Total Quality brings back spirit to the workplace. When I first brought up this point to an audience, I saw many disturbed faces. After my lecture more people came up to talk with me about this last advantage than all the others.

What do I mean by the return of the spirit. First, let me quote Ayn Rand about spirit:

> **"The quickest way to kill the human spirit is to ask someone to do mediocre work."**

When business and government were asking people not to do their best, they were telling the workers, in essence, to lie to their customers. Even though the workers knew they could have done better, they weren't supposed to. Because the old paradigm preached that to do it right the first time cost too much.

The cost that was never built into that statement was the cost of the workers' integrity. Not doing your best but presenting it as your best is a lie. And lying corrupts the soul.

Pirsig points out in his book that the closeness of the words *good* and *God, dharma* and *Buddha,* are not mistakes. And adds that the word *enthusiasm* comes from Greek, meaning "filled with the spirit of God."

All the major religions of the world—Confucianism, Hinduism, Judaism, Christianity, Buddhism, Islam—have some variation on the Golden Rule: Do unto others as you would have them do unto you.

The Total Quality movement operationalizes that rule. Do it right the first time. Do better tomorrow than you did today. Those imperatives sound very much like what is being asked by the major religions.

The quest for excellence is a way, without a compromise, to bring the spirit of God back into the workplace. This creates an entirely different validation of work, and it is something the Western world has not had at any time in this century.

> **To not quest for excellence might be considered sacrilege.**

I would submit that the Total Quality movement has brought back a direct connection between the religion you practice and the work you do. You can now live up to your religious beliefs even as you are fulfilling your daily work. And if you are not religious, it still works because of the direct and positive impact on the human spirit.

What are the implications of the adoption of this paradigm across the board in country after country? As near as I can tell, the results will closely approximate the descriptions of utopia.

Everything works right the first time.

Everyone quests for doing it better tomorrow than today.

Customer needs are constantly met.

Products work better, last longer.

Waste disappears from the system.

People love their jobs.

Sounds pretty good to me.

The quest for **excellence** automatically opens up the quest for **innovation**. Innovation takes us into territories we have never been to before; and therefore, to be responsible to the future and to the things we value, we must develop a sense of **anticipation** of the implications of our innovations. This will allow us to pick from the many potential solutions to our problems and find the few that best support those values we wish to carry into the future.

Here we see the three keys for the twenty-first century again: anticipation, innovation, excellence.

I can think of no more powerful example than the Total Quality management paradigm to show you what can happen when a paradigm changes. I would submit to you that the Total Quality management paradigm has created an epidemic of quality throughout the world. And any organization that doesn't catch this disease may have a very difficult time surviving the next twenty years.

The paradigm shift that Deming and Juran and Crosby and many others began is not just a revolution in manufacturing. It is a revolution in the human spirit. And if we continue along the road they have laid out, we will find that excellence must permeate every nook and cranny of our lives. It must impact on, not just what we use in our lives, but how we act in our lives—the warp and weft, the very fabric of how our lives are used.

For these reasons and many more, I predict that the Total Quality process will be hailed in the twenty-first century as the most important paradigm shift to come out of the twentieth century.

What is impossible to do, but if it could be done, would fundamentally change your business?

CHAPTER 10

Going Back to Zero

IT WOULD BE EASY to continue with examples, but it is time to begin to draw some lessons. The single most important lesson is captured in what I call the going-back-to-zero rule.

When a paradigm shifts, everyone goes back to zero.

By zero, I mean that regardless of what your position was with the old paradigm—number one in market share, leader in the technology, best reputation—you are back at the starting line with the new paradigm. Because of this change in leverage, the practitioners of the new paradigm have a chance to not just compete with but defeat the titans of the old paradigm.

There is a kind of conceptual democracy to this rule because it suggests that no one stays on top forever. It is like an election where the vote is determined not by past successes but future promise. It is this rule that explains the success of some entrepreneurs who have done amazingly well against the established and powerful.

IBM AND APPLE

One of the most dramatic examples of the back-to-zero effect can be found with the development and marketing of the personal computer. If I had written in 1975 that two young men, neither of whom had finished his college education, would create a computer in their garage that would force the IBM Corporation (which then held more than 60 percent of the world computer market) to drastically change, within five years, its methods of manufacturing, software production, sales, and machine security, how many of you would have taken me seriously?

But that's exactly what happened. Steve Jobs and Steve Wozniak did it when they created their Apple computer and its marketing strategy. Their rules were simple, brilliantly so.

When the Apple II came out in 1977, there is no question that people at IBM and other mainframe computer companies laughed. And yet, by 1982, almost all of them were trying to emulate Apple's paradigm.

Now, let's check my everybody-goes-back-to-zero thesis by setting down four rules that IBM was following in 1975 and which were crucial to their success:

1. IBM manufactured the heart of their computers, the microprocessor. In fact, IBM was one of the best at that in the world.

2. IBM always wrote the software for its computers using its own very talented software groups.

3. Without fail, IBM products were sold by IBM super salespeople, the best in the world at what they do.

4. No one was allowed to open up an IBM product except an IBM person. In some cases, to remove the cover of an IBM product voided the warranty.

IBM had other rules, too, but in the 1970s these four were clearly part of a successful IBM paradigm.

Then along came Apple. Jobs and Wozniak wanted to get into the personal computer business. And to do that, they created a new approach, a new model, a new paradigm. Let's take a look at their rules:

1. Since Apple couldn't afford to manufacture its own microprocessors for its little computers, it purchased them from an outside source.

2. Since Apple couldn't afford to hire a lot of software people to write programs, it hired a small software house, Microsoft, to help it write software.

3. Since Apple was a brand-new company and had only minimal salespeople, it sold its products through retail stores across the country.

4. To encourage broader use of its product, Jobs and Wozniak designed the Apple to be opened by the users

(in fact, they attached the top with pop-open fasteners to make taking it off easier) and put in empty card slots to invite the user to add new products from Apple **and other manufacturers** that would enhance the power and flexibility of the little computer.

What a dramatic difference between the IBM rules and Apple's rules. So how did IBM get into the personal computer market in 1982?

1. IBM did not manufacture the PC's microprocessor. Instead, it bought it from a vendor (just like Apple did).

2. IBM got key parts of its PC software written by a vendor just like Apple did. (Microsoft, to be exact, the same software house that helped Apple!)

3. IBM sold its PC through retailers like Sears, Computerland, and others (exactly the same way as Apple).

4. And, just like Apple, IBM made it easy for its customers to get inside the box, to access the empty slots waiting for others' equipment.

And Apple did it all first! Even mighty IBM who had its own powerful and successful computer paradigm had to switch to Apple's rules in order to play the new game. And the effects are not completed yet. Jobs and Wozniak have had quite an effect on one of the world's greatest companies simply by creating their new paradigm.

By the way, I am not being critical of IBM. On the contrary, I applaud its ability to step outside its own highly successful paradigm and adopt another paradigm in order to compete in this market. Someone at the top understood that when the rules change, IBM had to change, too. The company could not play the PC game with old IBM rules; it had to play the game with Apple rules.

Here is the key point in this discussion: Apple wrote the rules. They were a good set of rules that added up to a powerful new paradigm. The result was that others followed. With its rules, Apple defined a market that did not exist in 1975. It will be a $100-billion market by the turn of the century all because of a new paradigm.

THE SWISS WATCH INDUSTRY

Think about the Swiss watch story with which we started this book. The Swiss had dominated the world watch industry for more than sixty years. Every indication suggested that their domination would continue. Yet the electronic quartz movement put them back to zero. Everything they were good at became irrelevant. They made the most accurate gears in the world. It was irrelevant. They made the best bearings. Who cared. They manufactured the finest mainsprings. Unneeded. All the advantages they had accrued in the old paradigm were worthless in the new.

SOLAR ENERGY

Luz International is an electrical power generation company in East Los Angeles that produces electricity at eight cents per kilowatt hour using mirrors. The fuel is photons. The concave mirrors concentrate sunlight on an oil-filled tube. The oil is heated to 800-plus degrees Fahrenheit and then is used to steam water to drive the turbines. Look at who is getting put back to zero: the coal-fired power plants; the manufacturers of equipment for those coal-fired plants, such as the pollution control manufacturers; the unit trains used to carry coal to the coal-fired plants.

All of a sudden, the rules are very different. How good are you at making mirrors, coal companies of America?

TOTAL QUALITY

It's the same with the Total Quality movement. Old managers who used to tell the workers what to do and when to do it, are finding themselves irrelevant because the workers are now in self-managed work teams telling themselves what to do and when to do it. Almost everything that managers were good at is now unnecessary. They are back to zero. Small wonder most of the resistance to the Total Quality programs comes from the middle managers.

ELECTRONIC BOOKS

I was talking with a vice-president of a major publishing house about this point. He asked me, ''What could put us back to zero?'' I asked him if he had seen the new Sony Data Discman. He had not.

What are publishers good at? Buying rights to properties; editing those properties until they are worthwhile reading; designing the book jackets and setting the type; printing vast amounts of books at low cost; marketing the books; physically moving those books to the right places at the right time; collecting the moneys and paying the author the royalties.

The Sony Data Discman uses laser technology to read from a compact disc that has not music on it but words. It displays those words on a high-contrast Liquid Crystal Backlit screen. It can be read in any kind of light. One three-and-one-half-inch disc can hold more than eighty thousand pages of information! In the next five years the Data Discman will be improved with the ability to transcribe entire books on an empty disc via modem, to record and store specific sections from the disc identified by the reader, and to download those sections onto the reader's computer.

How does this impact the book industry? Printing as it is now known will be irrelevant. No paper needed. No presses needed. No binding needed.

Instead the Data Discman is the universal book. Insert a disc and read your book. Since the imaging hardware of the Discman determines the size and shape of the typography, no typesetting will be needed, either.

Because the Data Discman will be able to write on a blank compact disc, no physical distribution is needed, either. You simply call up the national bookseller who tells you to hook up your Discman to the phone; they then send the signals that the Discman inscribes on the blank disc. In seconds, you have your book. You are charged for the line time, the royalties to the author, the fee to the electronic distributor, and that's it. No trees cut down. No driving to the mall to visit the local B. Dalton. No trucks carrying books across the country. You get the idea.

And, remember, your Data Discman, which will weigh less

than a pound, can carry more than eighty thousand pages on one disc. If you have an eyesight problem, the Discman will be able to display type as large as necessary or display Japanese kanji or Chinese ideographs with the same ease as the alphabet.

Of course, not everything that publishers are good at is back to zero. But some of the elements they count on most to keep away the competition (cost of large press runs, for instance) will be irrelevant. In fact, their greatest power now resides in their staff's capabilities, not the hardware of the business.

You see here the power of the paradigm shift, once again, to put entire industries back to zero.

THE PARADIGM SHIFT QUESTION

There is a way to begin to connect yourself to what could put you back to zero. It is a question to be asked and it triggers discussion that leads to domains outside your boundaries.

> **What is impossible to do in your business (field, discipline, department, division, technology, etc.—just pick one), but if it could be done, would fundamentally change it?**

This question elicits delightful, creative answers, because it focuses your attention on two very important attributes. First, what is "**impossible**" takes you outside your boundaries. "Impossible" is a wonderful boundary word. This part of the question makes you step beyond. Second, "would **fundamentally**" suggests the level of change needed. Not trivial. Fundamental. When you put these two attributes together, I guarantee that you are talking about paradigm shifts.

Ask this question at all levels of your organization. Everyone will have an answer to it in the proper scale. Of course, sometimes someone is cute and answers, ''If we could beam people aboard . . .'' That's okay because they are stretching.

Test the utility of the impossibilities by asking if anyone knows of any early indicators in the real world that would suggest it might be possible.

I asked the question of Cray Computer's senior management team in the early 1980s. They knew the answer—parallel processing. Parallel processing is done by hooking up many small computers to run in parallel. Doing so would speed up the ability to compute while lowering costs by as much as 90 percent. But no one could do it.

Today you can buy parallel processing computers. By the mid-1990s parallel processing computers will dominate many segments of the supercomputer market. To recognize that impossibility a decade before it happened gave my clients time to prepare. And they did.

When I was working with a food company, and asked the question, a young food scientist answered, ''If we had a machine that you could just put the raw materials into—grain, oil, sugar, salt, yeast, whatever—and dial the food to be produced, it would change everything.''

It sure would. How many food companies are prepared to make the change required to produce this all-purpose food machine? If you ask are there any early indicators, just look at the Japanese bread-making machines.

Ask the question often, of everyone. Listen to the answers. It will keep you in touch with that strange space on the other side of your boundaries where you could be put back to zero.

To know what a paradigm is and how it changes is your best insurance against being put back to zero. Please understand, you can't stop the process. IBM could not have stopped the introduction of the personal computer. General Motors could not stop the spread of Total Quality manufacturing in the United States. The Swiss could not contain the development of the quartz watch.

By spotting such changes early, knowing what they are, you can then participate in the paradigm shift and begin the development process with the pioneers, thus helping guarantee that you will be a part of the new paradigm.

CHAPTER 11

Key Characteristics of Paradigms

NOW IT IS TIME to draw some conclusions about paradigms. There are seven characteristics that I think are important to understand, especially if you want to anticipate your own future better and improve your ability to innovate.

1. PARADIGMS ARE COMMON

Thomas Kuhn did not believe this when he wrote his book. In an interview in the May 1991 issue of *Scientific American,* he expressed a frustration with the way the paradigm theory has become looser and more generalized. I, too, have seen the idea used poorly. For instance, someone declares that a paradigm shift has occurred when only one rule of many comprising that paradigm has been changed. The boundaries are still the same; the measures of success are almost the same. One change in one rule does not constitute a paradigm shift. But if you stick to the definition I gave you in Chapter 3 of this book, I think you can see that paradigms abound in all phases of life from science to business to culture.

The big difference between scientific paradigms and all other paradigms is in the precision of measurement by which scientists "prove" their models. That plus the replication requirement gives them great power to build on one another's work.

But keep in mind, we measure for politeness and lawsuits and the straightness of a brick wall, too. We keep score of problems solved in all the paradigms we practice. It is just that most of our scoring is much more subjective and variable than scientific scoring.

You'll find that there are paradigms all around. Many are trivial; that is, the rules and regulations do not impact much, if at all, on the larger environment. But all paradigms great or small have the same effect of giving the practitioner special vision and understanding and specific problem-solving methods.

2. PARADIGMS ARE FUNCTIONAL

You may have concluded because of the many comments I have made about the effects of paradigms and their influence that I see paradigms as something undesirable. I don't. In fact, I don't know how human beings would get along without them. They are necessary. We need rules to help us live in this highly complex world. Without rules for direction, we would be constantly confused because the world is too rich with data.

Paradigms are functional because they help us distinguish data that is important from that which is not. The rules tell us how to look at the data and then how to deal with it.

Let me share an anecdote from my family life to illustrate this utility. My son, Andrew, watched me play tennis for many years, but, until he was fifteen, he wasn't interested in the game. Then he took some lessons. After he began playing, he said to me one day in passing, "I'm going to enjoy watching the U.S. Open with you this year." I asked him why. He said, "Now I know what to look for." Andy was learning the tennis paradigm. Before he took his lessons, when he had watched tennis all he saw on the TV screen was two people in white clothes running all over a green area hitting a fuzzy little white ball back and forth between them. But because he had no point of reference, no rules by which to understand and evaluate what they were doing, it was meaningless.

As he began to play the game, he learned the rules of tennis. He understood a drop shot, a topspin forehand, a slice backhand, a half volley, an overhead. He understood the concepts of strategy, and, all of a sudden, what was meaningless data for him before became understandable, interesting, and useful, as a direct result of learning a paradigm. We all experience that new understanding when we learn a paradigm.

When we gather in groups of people, whether they are businesses, organizations, cultures, we aggregate the problem-solving power that each of us has with our specific paradigms to deal with the larger world. With my paradigms, I can solve certain classes of problems. With your paradigms, you can solve another class of problems. It is our **diversity** as a group that lets us deal with the complexity of the world through the application of many paradigms. And that makes the group much more capable than any single individual of dealing with the world in the long run.

For that reason, whenever I hear people speak against immigrants of a different culture as "weakening" the United States, I object. Because I know that their differences have increased the potential problem-solving capacity of the nation. American immigration laws have stimulated and catalyzed this power of difference. Why would we ever want to give up such an advantage?

3. THE PARADIGM EFFECT REVERSES THE COMMONSENSE RELATIONSHIP BETWEEN SEEING AND BELIEVING

Remember the cliché "I'll believe it when I see it!" From what I have said in this book, you should conclude that the reverse is more accurate: **"I'll see it when I believe it."** In other words, subtle vision is preceded by an understanding of the rules. To see well, we need paradigms.

Every teacher sees this happen. I know I did. When I was explaining a concept to my students, many were unable to understand it even though the information was directly in front of them. But, as they began to understand the principles, they would say, one by one, "Oh, now I get it." What they were getting was the paradigm; what they were gaining was a significant change in vision.

This third point about paradigms is especially important for people who are employers. It explains why some new employees have a difficult time of adjustment. What they are really doing is adjusting to the paradigms of the organization, and, until they know those rules, they will literally be unable to see things that are obvious to people who have been there for a while. The temptation is to think that these people are not intelligent enough to handle the job. The fact is, they may have more than enough intelligence; they simply lack the understanding of the particular paradigm.

The other side of this situation offers a special opportunity for employers. Think back to the Marriott example I shared in Chapter 5. Your new employees don't know the rules, so they lack the ability to see things the way trained employees see them. On the other hand, with that fresh vision, they still have the ability to see things that are important, that can no longer be seen by those who have learned the organizational paradigms.

So, new employees are on both sides of the "seeing and believing" characteristic of paradigms. Treat them gently until they learn to see. Use their naïve perceptions to your advantage to see yourselves anew.

4. THERE IS ALMOST ALWAYS MORE THAN ONE RIGHT ANSWER

In his book, *Ascent of Man,* Jacob Bronowski writes about the impossibility of identifying the right answer: "There is no absolute knowledge, and those who claim it—whether they are scientists or dogmatists—open the door to tragedy. All information is imperfect. We have to treat it with humility" (page 353).

The effects of paradigms explain why this must be the case. By changing my paradigm, I change my perception of the world. That does not have to mean I must have contradictory perceptions; rather that I am seeing another portion of the world that is just as real as the portion that I saw with the other rules. But because one paradigm allows me access to one set of information and another paradigm allows me access to another set, I may end up with two different, yet equally correct, explanations of what is happening in the world.

Anyone who assumes there is only one right answer is missing the point of paradigms.

5. PARADIGMS TOO STRONGLY HELD CAN LEAD TO PARADIGM PARALYSIS, A TERMINAL DISEASE OF CERTAINTY

Paradigm paralysis is, unfortunately, an easy disease to get and is often fatal. More than a few organizations, which were dominant in their prime, have succumbed and died of it. It is a "hardening of the categories," so to speak. It grows from a situation of power. We all have our paradigms, but, when one is successful and in power, there is a temptation to take our paradigm and convert it into the paradigm. After all, isn't it what made us successful? Once we have **the** paradigm in place, then any suggested alternative has to be wrong. "That's not the way we do things around here." This problem can occur at all levels, in all organizations, and will, in the long run, throttle new ideas.

In nonturbulent times, absolute positions may not be immediately dysfunctional because change occurs more slowly. One set of rules may last a long time. But, in turbulent times, to have **the** right way to do things and no ability to explore alternatives is extremely dangerous. What was right six months ago could become wrong because of a major, rapid change in the environment.

Arthur C. Clarke writes in *Profiles of the Future,* a book first published in 1962 and recently reissued: "It is really quite amazing by what margins competent but conservative scientists and engineers can miss the mark when they start with the preconceived idea that what they are investigating is impossible" (page 21).

He said it in another way, too, which is now stated as Clarke's First Law: "When a distinguished but elderly scientist states that something is possible, he is almost certainly right. When he states that something is impossible, he is very probably wrong" (page 29).

Paradigm paralysis has profound implications for innovation within an organization. Why is it that internal innovation is so difficult to stimulate? Because **the** paradigm is already in place. So, until we can change that attitude and stimulate people to be more flexible and break out of their paradigms to search for alternatives, we will continue to find the great new ideas, on the whole, being discovered outside the prevailing institutions.

6. PARADIGM PLIANCY IS THE BEST STRATEGY IN TURBULENT TIMES

Paradigm pliancy is the opposite of paradigm paralysis. It is the purposeful seeking out of new ways of doing things. It is an active behavior in which you challenge your paradigms on a regular basis by asking the Paradigm Shift Question:

What do I believe is impossible to do in my field, but, if it could be done, would fundamentally change my business?

And then coupling it to the question:

Who, outside my field, might be interested in my unsolved problems?

These two questions will help you begin the search for your new paradigms, and by actively searching you greatly increase the likelihood of finding them.

When you hear something "crazy" about your field of expertise, follow up on it. When you run into data that contradicts what you know to be true, look carefully at it. Even if this data turns out to be truly crazy and wrong, the cultivation of an open attitude will pay off for you in the long run.

Here's a good first step toward paradigm pliancy. When someone goes **against** your paradigm, fight your natural tendency to explain why it is impossible and, instead, say:

"I never thought about it that way before, tell me more."

And, then, be quiet and listen. You'll be surprised at how many good ideas you will hear.

7. HUMAN BEINGS CAN CHOOSE TO CHANGE THEIR PARADIGMS

It is this observation about paradigms that makes me such an optimist about the future. Human beings are not genetically encoded with only one way of looking at the world. In fact, our coding seems to give us the capability to look at the world in a wide variety of ways.

If you are religious, this ability to change is called free will. If you are not, it's called self-determination. The result is the same—**you can choose to see the world anew**.

By the way, there is a corollary to observation 7: Since I've run into the paradigm concept, I've discovered that **there are very few irrational people in the world**.

When I am talking to someone who has a severe disagreement with my observations, I am on the alert for a disagreement, not of fact, but of paradigms. Almost always that is the explanation. The person is looking at the same things I'm looking at but using a different set of filters to examine the data, and, as a result, sees different things.

Kuhn suggested that you must consider, when talking to a person with a different paradigm, that you are talking to a person with a different language. Until you can speak their language, you will not be able to communicate clearly. I think that is excellent advice.

So, when I get into a disagreement, I've learned, I must quiet down and listen. Almost always the person will, sooner or later, tell me what his or her paradigm is. And, once I understand it, I can begin to understand what he or she is saying. I may still disagree, but at least I know why.

These seven aspects of the Paradigm Principles reinforce why this concept is so crucial for anticipating your future.

You lead between paradigms.

CHAPTER 12

Managers, Leaders, and Paradigms

IN THE PAST COUPLE OF YEARS people like Warren Bennis have been making important distinctions between managers and leaders. It is time we look at the Paradigm Principles to see what they have to say to both of these important roles.

For managers, I have already made some recommendations. I would like to add three more that I believe will improve your ability to stimulate better anticipation and innovation.

For those of you who would be leaders in your field, there is another set of recommendations. Because leadership is going to be so crucial in these next two decades, you will need to be clear on how paradigm shifts and leading are intertwined.

Let us begin with the management observations.

1. Managers must demonstrate paradigm pliancy if they are going to expect others to practice it.

Too many times I have visited with the workers and employees who tell me how they try to be innovative and offer new ideas only to get beaten up by their managers. The only way managers can convince the people who work for them to break the rules is to demonstrate their willingness to support that kind of behavior. That is exactly what the general manager of the Marriott Hotel in Burlington, Massachusetts did. He showed by his openness, his invitation, that he wanted people to step outside the boundaries and find new ways to solve old problems.

And that is exactly what didn't happen to the woman in the research lab (Chapter 5) who was told she was too new to have a ''big'' idea.

The more active managers can be in the search for new paradigms, the more likely those managers will be to have people searching with them and for them.

I was visiting with some Upjohn executives in the spring of 1991 and Jack A. Sharrock, executive director of Corporate Business Development, made a very useful point about letting people step outside the boundaries. We ended up drawing the little schematic you see in Figure 15 to represent what he was saying.

Two basic things happen when you step outside the boundaries. The first is that you find you are able to apply the prevailing paradigm rules effectively in a new, uncharted area (A). In other words, you have extended the domain of the old paradigm. More problems to solve with the rules you are so good at.

That is what happened in the 1970s with the piston engine

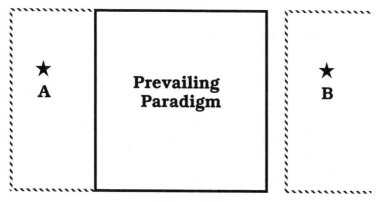

Figure 15

paradigm. Remember how everyone was saying piston engines were dead because they believed the engines to be incompatible with environmental and energy efficiency standards? But, once the engine engineers stepped outside their old boundaries, they found that, with the help of electronics, they could keep their piston engines and solve a whole new set of problems with the prevailing paradigm.

The second option is the one we have been talking about throughout this book: You find that your employee has stepped into a new domain (B) that will require a new paradigm to solve the problems in it.

So it turns out that you have nothing to lose. Either way you find out something important. But you, the manager, must create the attitude.

2. Managers must facilitate and encourage cross talk.

Cross talk is having people from different disciplines, from different departments, from different divisions, talk about their problems together. This kind of "managing" is crucial because, more and more, we are going to find the answers to our problems by applying someone else's paradigms.

The idea is to increase the understanding of one another's problems. The hope is that perhaps several weeks or several months later, the person who knows of a problem outside his field will come across a piece of data or a new idea for a tool. They will remember the other person's problem and tell him about this possible new solution.

At Motorola, they call this "managing the white space," the space between the divisions that no one crosses. To be a successful company in the twenty-first century, you had damn well better cross that white space!

3. By listening to all those screwy ideas, managers gain a special leverage for innovation.

Jerry Allan, an architect and chairman of the Visual Studies Program at the Minneapolis College of Arts and Design, says, "Everything important in the twenty-first century will be hyphenated." And this is the advantage of managers with open doors to wild ideas. Remember I said back in Chapter 4 that it took a hundred crazy ideas before the really good one shows up. Well, it's time to modify that statement a little. I was talking about ideas in isolation.

But something else also happens. You are listening to idea number 5. It sounds really strange. But when the person leaves, you thank him for his thoughts and invite him to come back anytime. Because you want to get to the one hundredth.

And idea number 37 was a real doozy, too. But again, in all

sincerity, you thank the would-be problem solver for her efforts.

And idea number 66. Funny. Useless. Except . . . you remember numbers 37 and 5 and when you put those three together, you have a really powerful idea! Hyphenation!

How many people heard those sixty-six ideas? Maybe only one person in the world. The managers who listen for connections can generate great and unique leverage for their companies. But it requires constant attention and an open mind.

AND NOW ABOUT LEADERSHIP

I have to thank Linda Dunbar from Hewlett-Packard who challenged me in the summer of 1988. She called me and asked me to participate in a Leadership Issues Forum. I said I didn't do "leadership" and that she ought to get Warren Bennis.

She told me that paradigms and leadership went hand in hand and she was surprised I didn't realize that.

We all experience our own kinds of paradigm paralysis. And I had it here. She forced me to think about this question: What is the relationship between paradigm shifting and leadership?

First let me give you my definition of a leader:

> **A leader is a person you will follow to a place you wouldn't go by yourself.**

I looked at a lot of definitions that ended up listing characteristics but didn't get to the heart of leadership. The list of characteristics explains why they are followed. Please note that my definition is neutral. Hitler fulfilled my definition because many Germans followed him to a place—the Nazi party— they wouldn't have gone to by themselves.

Keeping the definition in mind, think about these two statements:

> **You manage within a paradigm.**
> **You lead between paradigms.**

That is the relation of paradigms to leadership. What allows you to ''manage'' within a paradigm? The rules, the guiding principles, the system, the standards, the protocols. Give a good manager the system and a manager will optimize it. That is a manager's job. It is called **paradigm enhancement**.

Paradigm enhancement is taking the rules and making them better. It is working your way up the B Phase of the Paradigm Curve. We spend 90 percent of our lives doing just this, because it is a form of progress and is the natural route to improvement. We also call it evolution. Paradigm enhancement is what the Total Quality movement is all about. To be able to paradigm enhance is crucial to success and is the domain of the manager.

But you don't manage between paradigms. Remember, leaving one paradigm while it is still successful and going to a new paradigm that is as yet unproven looks very risky. But leaders, with their intuitive judgment, assess the seeming risk, determine that shifting paradigms is the correct thing to do, and, because they are leaders, instill the courage in others to follow them.

This kind of change, paradigm shift change, occurs during less than 10 percent of our lives. Yet, it is as important as the paradigm enhancing that consumes the other 90 percent. I don't say it is more important, but it is surely equal.

To be successful in the twenty-first century, you will need to be competent at both these kinds of changes for your organization to flourish. One without the other will not work.

Paradigm shifting without the follow-on skills of paradigm enhancing leaves you vulnerable to the paradigm pioneers who practice Total Quality. Paradigm enhancement without the skills of paradigm shifting will lead you to continually improve obsolete products and services. Nobody will buy obsolete excellence.

Therefore you need to know about, understand, and utilize both kinds of change.

This book should be helpful to leaders because after reading it they will understand more clearly the phenomena they are dealing with. But it is not, nor can it ever be, a description of how to "manage" a shift of paradigms. Leaders lead to new paradigms in a myriad of ways. Depending on conditions, depending on the kinds of people following, each paradigm shift will require different pathways to get to the next paradigm.

After having watched paradigms change in organizations for almost twenty years, I have seen an interesting pattern of choices that occurs during a paradigm shift. It is really an oscillation between shifting paradigms and changing customers. Here are the three patterns in order of ascending impact:

Keep your paradigm; change your customer.

Change your paradigm; keep your customer.

Change your paradigm; change your customer.

Again and again I have watched companies struggle with these choices. Each has advantages and disadvantages. The first choice allows you to internally keep doing what you are good at.

Deluxe Corporation (formerly Deluxe Check Printers) has been following the first pattern—keep your paradigm; change your customer. They have been the industry leader in check printing. They do it faster, with more accuracy, than anyone else. But all trends in electronic banking suggest the days of check writing are numbered, so Deluxe started looking for other customers who could use a printer that was very fast and error-free. Now they are printing bank forms, office forms, computer forms, and their biggest diversification in 1987 was into direct-mail greeting cards. In all of these cases, their ability to put ink on paper is fundamental to their success. In the process, they have many new customers who never knew them before.

By the way, Deluxe has also gotten into the electronic funds transfer business, so they are also trying to keep their old customers, too.

IBM followed the second dictum—change your paradigm; keep your customer—and ventured into personal computers. They wanted to prevent their corporate clients from deserting them and going to Apple or Radio Shack for their desktop computers.

Gould, Inc., tried the third route—change your paradigm; change your customer—and failed. They had been a great battery company but their CEO saw a wonderful opportunity in the computer chip market. He walked away from their core business and toward a business that, had they succeeded, would have been much bigger than the one they were in. But they failed.

Motorola, Inc., on the other hand, led by Bob Galvin as CEO, made an amazingly successful "change your paradigm—change your customer" move that began in 1964.

Galvin was visiting a dealer and heard that dealer explain to his son that "the power is in the hands of the buyer." In a letter describing his decision, Mr. Galvin wrote, "When I heard him say that, all of the frustrations that we were seeing in the consumer appliance business clarified." And he resolved to get out of that business.

It took Motorola until 1974 to complete the transition. By making that change, he created the environment and the potential from which grew Motorola's world-class position in semiconductors which created a new customer base.

Leaders need to be aware of these choices. In these kinds of change-situations only leaders, not managers, can succeed.

I am not knocking people who can only manage. We need them badly once we are within the new paradigm. But we need to recognize that someone can be a great manager and a lousy leader.

Of course, the reverse is equally true—someone can be a

lousy manager and a great leader. We would all like that wonderful combination of leader-manager, but they are rarer than we would like to believe.

Warren Bennis set forth a list of characteristics of leaders in the May 1990 issue of *Training* magazine. It is instructive to look at some of those in light of what I have just said:

The manager administers; the leader innovates.

The manager has a short-range view; the leader has a long-range perspective.

The manager asks how and when; the leader asks what and why.

The manager has his eye on the bottom line; the leader has his eye on the horizon.

The manager accepts the status quo; the leader challenges it.

Within the context of our paradigm discussion, the Bennis characteristics fit beautifully. Look how he links leadership to boundaries, to new horizons.

This is exactly what John Opel and Frank Carey did for IBM when they pushed their company into the personal computer business. And Thomas Watson, Jr., did it for IBM when he pushed his electrical engineers into the transistor age.

Roger Milliken, CEO of Milliken and Company, a privately held textile company headquartered in Spartanburg, South Carolina, demonstrated true leadership when he began his company's drive to world-class status in the early 1980s. Experts were predicting the demise of the United States textile industry, but at Milliken, through a relentless pursuit of excellence, it has been just the opposite. That the company won the Malcolm Baldridge Award in 1990 is a testament to the leadership exhibited by Roger Milliken and the rest of his team.

And this isn't just about official leaders. Many times paradigm shifts are driven by people who take a leader's role when no one else is doing it. You could not have guessed who these people would be before they show up.

Ralph Nader is a perfect example of just such a person. No official credentials qualified him to challenge the entire automotive industry. But he did. He changed one of the oldest paradigms—"let the buyer beware"—and turned it inside out. Now he is the official leader of the consumer movement, but that is not where he started.

One final note: Visionaries are not necessarily leaders. How can you tell the difference? Visionaries have great ideas about the future. But when they look behind them, no one else is following. Leaders always have people behind them.

Most leaders are not visionaries. But all leaders know who the visionaries are and select, from them, the great ideas that they want to lead to.

We all have our roles. Some of us are visionaries. Some are leaders. Some are managers. Some, followers. Some of us, few in number, are combinations of all four roles. Once in a very great while you will come upon a visionary-leader-manager; but it is not a requirement to have one to get to the future. We just need to have teams made up of all of these people—visionaries, leaders, and managers—and do the best we can in our roles.

This team approach will be the hallmark of the great companies of the twenty-first century. I am convinced of it.

And then again, maybe it could happen.

CHAPTER 13

Shifts for the 1990s—a Barker's Dozen

IN CHAPTER 2, I said that almost all major trends are triggered by a paradigm shift or a set of paradigm shifts. Before I share with you what I think will be some of the most important paradigm shifts of the last decade in the twentieth century, let me reflect on a set of major trends started by paradigm shifts in the 1980s.

TRENDS FOR THE 1990S

1. The regionalization of world economics. Too many people are talking globalization as if that is the only way to go in the 1990s. But the trend I see is Western Europe forming an economic unit; Eastern Europe working toward joining that regional group; and Canada, the United States, and Mexico setting up structures to create a regional economic unit. These constitute

171

new boundaries with new rules needed for success—a paradigm shift. Japan is trying to position itself to function in both these units even as it increases its loans and other aid to Asian neighbors. I don't see globalization nearly as likely as regionalization for the next two decades.

2. The greening of industry. The paradigm shift began in the 1960s, and in the 1990s it will reach full flower. Company after company is finding that, instead of resisting recycling and reducing outflow of pollution, it is smarter and cheaper to do just the opposite. Led by companies like 3M and McDonald's, the businesses of the world will drive this trend to culmination by the end of this decade.

3. Quality everywhere. I have described the potency of the paradigm shift behind this trend in Chapter 9. I believe it will be the norm by 1999.

4. Celebration of diversity. This trend is being triggered by a paradigm shift in human resources. Driven by the feminist paradigm shift and the minorities movement, slowly but steadily we are learning that variety is the greatest strength. This human understanding is being supported by exactly the same observations in the area of natural environment. It is my expectation that during the 1990s, the United States will document the great advantages it has received through its massive immigration policy that has driven diversity in this nation.

5. Gambling instead of taxes. The paradigm shift behind this trend is the new political landscape that requires politicians to claim they are not raising taxes even as they extract more money from the public. This is a dangerous trend, I believe, because state-run gambling to replace taxes undermines the requirement in a democracy that its citizens make choices about how their taxes are raised and distributed to support the public will. Gambling reinforces the concept of luck and fate as the mechanisms for distributing the bounty of the world and subverts the idea that hard work and learning pay off.

Hard choices require hard work. Gambling run by the state to pay for state needs is wrong for a democracy. Period. (It's obvious what my values paradigm is, isn't it?)

6. The fiber optics everywhere. Fiber optics with its enormous capacity to carry messages of all sorts—voice, data, visual—represents a paradigm shift in communications. Its installation during the 1990s will accelerate and will impact on TV networks, cable systems, office communications, the entertainment industry, the publishing industry. Even the health care and education sectors will be dramatically impacted by this trend. All because the cost and ease of moving data is improved by magnitudes with fiber optics.

7. Energy conservation optimized. The paradigm shift started in the 1970s, was ignored in the late 1980s, and will come back now to be completed in the 1990s. Later in this chapter, I will describe a major paradigm shift that will drive this trend, but it is already moving well enough.

8. National health care. The forces are in play. The old paradigm is failing. Costs per problem solved are skyrocketing. This trend is just beginning. It will take two decades to be fulfilled but during the last decade of this century, it will begin its ascent. Too many people in this country cannot afford health care as it is now configured. Corporations are now seeing that they cannot fight the battle of costs operating as separate islands against the health care sector. The wellness paradigm shift is waiting to be actualized. The Canadian system offers an alternative model that the United States can adapt. This is the decade it should happen.

9. Self-managing work teams. Connected to the Total Quality trend but worth mentioning by itself. This is an important trend because of the way it democratizes the workplace. It is important because it displaces one of the largest groups of the middle class—the middle manager. The challenge will be to find jobs for the middle managers who will no longer be managing.

10. Water as precious. By the end of the 1990s, water will be dealt with in a very different way than it is today. In the water-rich state of Minnesota, it costs about two dollars to buy an acre-foot of water. (An acre-foot is one acre of flat land flooded to one foot of depth with water.) In Arizona, that same acre-foot in 1990 cost eighty-eight cents to purchase. Minnesotans help subsidize Arizonans with the national taxes so that Arizonans can buy water cheaper than Minnesotans can. The water subsidies are going to disappear. The real cost of water will make the Southwest and the West fundamentally change how they use and reuse their water.

11. Biotechnology everywhere. This one is obvious but we should note it because of its growing impact. In 1991 the biotechnology we see is equivalent to Wilbur and Orville Wright and their airplane. We are impressed with flights of a couple hundred yards. By the end of the 1990s, we will begin to see the biotechnological equivalents of 747s. Biotechnology, a scientific paradigm shift, has applications not only in medicine and agriculture but in polymer manufacture, computer chip design, education, and energy. This is as close to a universal tool as you can get and we will see universal applications.

12. Intellectual property as the key to wealth. Doing more and more with less and less was a Buckminster Fuller prescription of the future. For the United States, where paradigm shifts abound and diversity of new ideas is standard, this trend is extremely positive. But, in order to benefit from it, the United States must take a very strong stand on the protection of intellectual property. When a designer spends five years to develop a beautiful table lamp and then someone in Taiwan can knock it off in a matter of hours with a CAD/CAM system and then import it back into the United States with no penalty or no payment to the designer, something is very wrong.

Corporations steal videotapes (I know because it has happened to me) to save a few bucks and then complain when someone in another country cheats on their patents. The lever of the twenty-first century will be information and ideas, America's greatest strength. If we want to take advantage of this trend, then we had better get to work developing clear and fair ways to protect this most ephemeral of all properties.

Those are the trends I think are especially important for the 1990s. Now let me share with you the paradigm shifts that I think will have major impact on the United States and the world.

NEW PARADIGMS FOR THE 1990S

1. Solar/hydrogen/fission. I combine these three elements because it will be the set that changes the energy equation. Remember, I have already stated that as a trend energy conservation will be a standard. Now, the question is what will be our source of fuel.

First, solar: Already described in Chapter 10 is how Luz International is producing electrical energy via mirrors. We need to add to that description the fact that they produce energy at eight cents a kilowatt hour. If they had enough demand, they could do it for six cents a kilowatt hour. At six cents, they are directly competitive with costs of building a new coal or nuclear plant that meets EPA standards.

Then there are the windmills. In the proper locations, they, too, are now cost-competitive with old paradigm technologies.

Add to the above the breakthroughs that Texas Instruments has made with their silicon bead photovoltaic cells—low-cost, rugged, reliable, easy-to-manufacture—and you can see that the revolution in solar energy is almost upon us.

But electricity by itself doesn't solve a lot of the nation's energy problems. You need a fuel that can be used to propel airplanes and trains and buses and cars. That is where hydrogen fits in: when you burn hydrogen molecules—H_2—with Oxygen you get H_2O. Water is not a bad pollutant. (You do get some hydroxiles, too, but in very small and manageable amounts.) Hydrogen makes a great fuel. To make hydrogen, right now, requires electricity. And our solar systems can give us that.

So where does fission fit into all of this? Isn't fission dead as a dodo bird? Nope. Our nuclear engineers, learning from some of their very stupid past mistakes, have come up with some new designs. Known as "supersafe," the reactors, by design, cannot go critical. No meltdowns possible.

And the engineers don't just say this: It is possible to safely test their designs to make sure their claims are true. The Swedes, who are shutting down all their reactors, have designed a super-safe reactor. And Argonne Labs, a government lab, has designed a ''breeder'' reactor that not only is supersafe but also reburns any plutonium it creates right in the very same reactor, thus removing the need for it ever to leave the nuclear plant. It eliminates the possibility that terrorists or a government will collect enough plutonium to make atomic bombs.

Fission produces no CO_2 (carbon dioxide). Fission requires minimum disturbance of the planet's surface. By burning down the radioactive material in the reactor, the waste materials are minimized, especially when compared with coal. It can provide the baseload for the first half of the twenty-first century until all the energy needs can be met by solar and conservation.

2. Time taxes. The earliest indicator of this paradigm shift has occurred in Littleton, Colorado. There, in 1990, a new program was born to lift the property tax burden off the elderly while gaining help for the schools.

The process is simple: Senior citizens go to the schools in the area and do various jobs. They help in the kitchen; they read to children in the classrooms; they monitor the bathrooms; they do calling to find out about absentees. In exchange, they are paid by having their property taxes reduced.

The results so far have been impressive. The senior citizens in the program have praised it for letting them keep their homes while providing meaningful help to the community. The school officials feel that they are actually getting more than their money's worth from this program because of how effective the seniors are.

And the children are gaining new friends from another generation—something America has almost lost in its cultural structure.

The question now becomes: Who else should be eligible for paying their taxes with time. How about those on welfare? How about those who have been laid off and don't want to lose their homes? How about the students themselves? Maybe they can go shovel the snow in front of the homes of the elderly who then come to school to help with the students' education.

This paradigm shift could bring new meaning to the hallowed phrases "Of the people, by the people, for the people."

3. The Buffalo Commons. The great plains are known for their incredible production of foodstuffs—grains and cattle. Frank and Deborah Popper, researchers at Rutgers University, predict "large chunks of the rural West will be abandoned and eventually drift into public or quasi-public holdings." (*The Christian Science Monitor*, December 18, 1990). Enormous amounts of land in the West have fewer than six people per square mile. It is virtually empty.

So the Poppers suggest that the land be accumulated and returned to its natural state, "The Buffalo Commons."

This image flies in the face of the irrigated and cultivated look that the states of Kansas, Nebraska, Montana, North and South Dakota now have.

The Poppers suggest that "preservation uses such as tourism, recreation, and retirement will become primary; extractive ones such as ranching, farming, logging, and mining—including for oil—will become secondary." Instead, much along the lines of the vision of Wes Jackson's Land Institute in Salinas, Kansas, the native flora and fauna would be reseeded and the buffalo and other species would be allowed to return and flourish.

Jackson has studied the richness of the prairie and the wealth of seeds that could be harvested from the natural prairie flora. What most people don't understand is that the prairie was not just one monocrop of buffalo grass. It was a complex ecology with many seed plants as part of that ecosystem. Jackson believes that it is possible to harvest those seeds. It will require new kinds of machinery (the new tools of the new paradigm) and new procedures, but he calculates that the living prairie—unplowed and unstructured—could produce significant foodstuffs economically without resorting to the old plow-up-the-land-and-plant-monocrops farming paradigm.

The Buffalo Commons is a paradigm shift within the agricultural community. And clearly the proponents are outsiders. One of the driving forces will be the reductions in tax subsidies for production of wheat and meat that then must be stored and sold by the federal government. Taxpayers will no longer support such subsidies if it means their taxes must escalate.

Think of it: Hundreds of thousands of buffalo thundering across the plains from Canada to Kansas once again. Sounds impossible, doesn't it?

4. Education K through competence. How slowly we learn. But now we have begun to understand the real goal of education. Not eighteen and out with a mediocre education, but stay as long as you need to, to become competent to be a citizen/worker of the twenty-first century.

The old rules were simple: States and localities paid schools to teach students until they were eighteen or nineteen years of age. After that, the per-student payment disappeared. Clear boundaries. But now, the United States is facing up to the fact that many of our "graduated" students cannot read, write, or compute. The value of their high school diploma, in the real world of competition, is zero.

Leading indicators of this K–competence movement can be seen in school districts like Wayzata, Minnesota, which gives a guarantee of performance for all its high school graduates. If those students don't live up to specific performance levels, the school system will "retrain" them until they do. No cost to employers. No cost to the kids.

To compete with the world in the twenty-first century, the United States cannot afford to have anything less than competence. The new rules are being written even as you read this.

5. Magical, mystical polymers. Ah, plastics. So much promise. So much left to be fulfilled. The paradigm shift in these materials will impact almost every aspect of society.

For instance, plastics are now being treated so that they can carry electricity better than copper. By arranging the molecules in a parallel orientation, Paul Smith of the University of California at Santa Barbara has created plastics with the potential for better than ten times the strength and stiffness of steel!

These polymers give us the capability to build bridges, buildings, cars, and other "strength" structures out of plastic. It may be possible to construct an electric automobile whose fenders are also the batteries.

Think about it: nonrusting, electricity conducting, color-embedded or transparent, electricity insulating depending on the specific plastic.

Even computer chips may be fabricated out of special polymers. Bruce Novak, a chemist at the University of California at Berkeley (boy, aren't those Californians interested in polymers!) found a polymer in late 1990 that can be turned into a conductor just by shining ultraviolet light on it. That opens the door for using some variation of this material as the coating on computer chips, to make the electrical connections between the transistors.

The cascade of innovations that will come from the revolution in polymers will spill across industries and around the world.

6. Nature's wisdom. The stories keep accumulating. That's how I collect my indicators. And, more and more, it is clear we have grossly underestimated the intelligence of our animal and plant cousins.

Kanzi, a pygmy chimp, has learned a vocabulary the equivalent of that of a two-year-old child. Kanzi creates unique sentences that indicate he knows what he is doing. He also understands spoken English and can respond to such complex commands as "Go get the lettuce in the microwave."

By the age of six he had a vocabulary of ninety symbols (he

pushes buttons on a symbol board to indicate the word he is using) and an understanding of two hundred spoken words.

But animal intelligence is in more than language skills. In a *Science News* article of November 3, 1990, researchers reported on examples of animals self-medicating themselves with natural pharmaceuticals.

Examples include a chimpanzee who was observed to have a significant intestinal illness chewing on a plant whose extracts are used to treat a variety of human ailments. Coincidence? The plant is rarely eaten by these chimps, and this chimp didn't eat the plant but rather sucked and swallowed only the bitter juice of the stem after chewing on it.

Sick monkeys and birds also have been observed eating plants that later were identified as medicinal in nature. But perhaps the most amazing example in the story was told by Holly T. Dublin, an ecologist who spent most of 1975 tracking a pregnant elephant in Kenya.

As reported in *Science News,* this elephant had almost never varied her daily routine. But, one day, she walked twenty-eight kilometers to a riverbank, stopped in front of a small tree, and ate it all. Only a short stump was left after her meal.

This tree was not part of her usual menu. In fact, the tree was not even part of the ecology of the elephant's daily life.

Four days later the elephant gave birth. Dublin discovered later on that pregnant women in Kenya brew a tea from the bark of that kind of tree to induce labor or abortion.

It is unbelievable to think that animals know which plants produce the right chemicals to help them cure disease and sickness and induce labor, isn't it?

How about plants doing the same thing? This data is far more substantiated. Biochemists have shown that plants send chemical signals to their fellow plants to stimulate those plants to produce insect-thwarting compounds called proteinase inhibitors.

I quote from an article in *Science News* of December 22, 1990: "The results offer a biochemical basis for a previously unrecognized form of defense gene regulation involving interplant communication."

Wait a minute? Interplant communication? Yes. It looks like when a plant is attacked by insect predators, it signals the other plants to produce species-specific toxins, to ward off the attack on themselves. It's like, "Well, they got me but they don't have to get you."

You wonder how much more we don't have a clue about, how many of nature's rules we have yet to begin to fathom?

7. Negawatts. I loved the word the first time I saw it. Turns the other word inside out, doesn't it? It is a word coined by the paradigm shifter of energy, Amory Lovins. Lovins, a trained physicist, began his paradigm shifting on electrical power utilities back in the 1970s.

He's at it again. The basic assumption behind Negawatts is that the United States can reduce its electrical energy consumption by up to 70 percent with no loss in quality of life. All of this can be had by just applying the appropriate and **presently available** energy conserving technologies.

Lovins loves to point out such facts as the following: that since 1979 the United States has obtained seven times as much new energy from energy efficiency as from all expansion of supply.

As a result of that energy savings, America has reduced its energy bill by about $150 billion per year. And there's far more left to be saved according to Lovins.

He focuses on electricity because it is the costliest form of energy and arguably the most damaging to the environment. Let me quote from his *Mother Jones* article of April 1991:

"It is now possible to save a quarter of our electricity by improving our lighting systems, a quarter in motors, and another quarter in everything else, by fully using the best technologies now on the market." And no laboratory prototypes are needed. You can buy all the stuff right now.

Lovins suggests that if we offer the right incentives to the power utilities, they will make these changes themselves. What are the proper incentives? Let them make a higher return on investment for energy savings than energy production. This idea was tested in New England in 1988 when the Northeast Utilities were put into a show-us-why-it-won't-work dilemma by the Connecticut Public Utilities Commission. The commission forced the utility to hire the Boston-based Conservation Law Foundation to teach them how to conserve.

End result: Northeast Utilities had been projecting a

5-percent growth rate in electricity, which required them to build a new plant immediately. Now they expect the growth in demand to decline by at least half, at an average cost of just six cents for each kilowatt hour saved—substantially less than the cost of new electricity.

Lovins has calculated that "good programs to save commercial and industrial electricity cost only about a half cent per kilowatt hour, which is several-fold cheaper than just operating a coal or nuclear plant, and ten to twenty times cheaper than building a new one" (Amory Lovins, "Negawatts," *Across the Board*, September 1990, page 22).

Remember when I said that new paradigms typically solve the unsolvable problems of the old paradigm and do it cheaper. Well, applying Lovins's Negawatts paradigm ends up also solving the carbon dioxide problem for the world! And it will generate up to $200 billion per year in net profits for those instituting the program!

I know. Too good to be true. Just look back to the other paradigm shifts that were disbelieved before you take too inflexible a position.

8. New building materials. I am always on the lookout for breakthroughs in building materials. Shelter is lacking for many in the third world. And even in the first world, we have too many people either homeless or living in homes that don't really give shelter.

I offer two examples. There is the house made of sand. Or almost sand. In Orlando, Florida, a company called Terra Block Worldwide knows how to mass-produce adobe blocks. The inventor of the process, Robert Gross, is a former NASA engineer and tinkerer.

He designed a machine that breaks all the rules for making adobe. The old paradigm was simple: Mix up some mud with a little straw blended in. Push it into forms. Wait for the mud to solidify and pull off the form. Bake in the sun for seven days.

Robert Gross didn't think that was the only way to do it. He realized that the sun was used to bake out the water. He asked himself if there was another way to get water out. His answer: squeezing.

So he built a machine that takes dirt and squeezes adobe blocks with a high-pressure hydraulic ram. Each block is twelve by ten by four inches and weighs about thirty pounds. His machine produces up to six hundred blocks an hour. And the cost per block, in terms of energy, is three tenths of one cent. Compared with any other building material on the market today, that is twenty times cheaper.

So far the company has not found any soil that won't work. Florida soil is the worst because of its high content in sand. Africa has the best.

Think of the long-term implications. For instance, the United States could give these machines away as foreign aid. One per village in the third world. The villagers provide the soil and the effort to stack the blocks. Schools. Hospitals. Homes. All from ''squeeze'' blocks. It could be the same in the United States. Replace ramshackle homes of the poor with adobe homes. The owner puts in sweat equity in exchange for the use of the machine. And it obviously can be used for standard housing anywhere with a waterproof coating on the blocks.

Example number two: growing structures beneath the sea. I had heard about this paradigm shift back in the 1970s but good data was hard to come by. Only recently did I get reconnected with the technology. The discoverer of the process is Wolf Hilbertz, an architect. He had some old World War I research done by Germans who were trying to extract gold from seawater to pay off the national debt. They were unsuccessful because of a hard crust that formed on the electrically charged probes they had immersed in the sea to collect the gold.

In perfect paradigm pliant fashion, Wolf wondered not about the gold but about the hard crust. So he replicated the experiment but put a wire mesh in place of the electrodes. The result was an encrusted wire mesh strong enough to be structural.

The material is like limestone and can withstand more than four thousand pounds of pressure per inch. It doesn't weaken when dried. What is this stuff? The equivalent of coral. And now, under the auspices of the United Nations, experimenters are "growing" bricks, tiles, pipes, to see how cheap and how effective it can be.

All that is required is steel mesh plus very low levels of electricity. The production time is measured in weeks not months. Environmental impact is nil; the fish are not bothered by the weak electrical charge and the total amount of material taken from the ocean's water is minimal.

These two examples are paradigm-shifting ways to deal with the building-material needs of the world. Both break the old rules

and offer huge potential for solving problems cheaply and effectively.

9. Gaia. The earth is alive and she is named Gaia. This is
the revolutionary thesis, a paradigm shift, offered by Robert
Lovelock in his book *The Ages of Gaia.*

Lovelock's background reads like a paragon of a paradigm
shifter. He is a biologist and chemist and an important inventor of
measuring instruments. It was early in his career that he was
given the opportunity to look at the earth in a new way. NASA
hired him to figure out how to determine if there was life on
Mars. To figure out how to determine the answer, Lovelock
found himself asking that question about the earth. What are the
key measures one could take that would prove, irrefutably, that
there was life on earth.

This exercise gave him a chance to view the earth as an alien
might. And he discovered many indicators that spoke to the life
of the planet. Chemical imbalance of the atmosphere, an extremely stable temperature, and other such measures.

From this experience, he came to what he called an ''intuitive'' conclusion: that the planet was, in aggregate, alive. That
all the individual living organisms were part of a larger integrated
organism we have called the biosphere, the living earth. And that
was the only way, integrated and inclusive, that life could inhabit
a planet—it had to be all or nothing.

Since then, Lovelock has fleshed out this paradigm. He
believes that the plant and animal life control both the earth's
climate, by regulating atmospheric carbon dioxide, and the bulk

composition of the atmosphere by controlling molecular nitrogen and molecular oxygen. The key elements of his thesis are:

1. The planetary temperature has been amazingly stable over a very long time even though the sun has increased its light energy output by almost 40 percent.

2. There is a richness of life at every level.

3. There seem to be mechanisms that actively create ideal conditions for life: oxygen production systems; CO_2-absorbing systems to prevent the planet from overheating; salt-capturing systems that keep the ocean from becoming toxic; support systems that embrace varieties of life.

This revolutionary thesis has been challenged by scientists who say that Lovelock is suggesting the planet "thinks" and is "conscious." To which Lovelock replies that the planet doesn't necessarily have to be conscious to create the systems necessary to make it a perfect place for life.

He also likes to point out that human beings are an assemblage of hundreds of billions of cells, each an entity, but whose sum total is something very alive, very special, and singular. Is it so crazy to think that the same pattern could be repeated at a planetary scale?

This new paradigm is forcing biologists and geologists to fundamentally readdress perceptions of the planet. It is in line with the ecological paradigm shift that has already taken place and also creates a potential connection to the major religions of the world.

10. Loans to the third world poor. How many of you

knew that in most parts of the world it is almost impossible for women to get loans? That is the prevailing paradigm of credit in the world.

And, obviously, male or female, if you are poor, you are a poor credit risk.

Not so under the rules of the new credit paradigm. The first and most important rule is: **The poor of the world are credit-worthy.** That axiom, by itself, is revolutionary. The rest of the system, first developed in Bangladesh, is simple: Groups of five people get together to ask for individual loans. The group guarantees all the loans. That means if one person doesn't make his or her monthly payment, the others must make it for them. The peer pressure structure has been reflected in a 99-percent repayment on loans in the program, a better repayment percentage of loans than almost any traditional bank loans.

The loans are small and periodic. Monthly, usually. And the interest rates match world rates. This last rule is much, much better than the poor have ever had before. Typically, if a poor person had borrowed from a local loan shark, he or she would have paid as high as 10 percent per day!

The results of this program are startlingly positive. In one example in Honduras, a woman who learned shoemaking was able, using the Women's World Banking Loans, to increase her business (at $200 per loan, through nine loans) from $10,890 in sales annually to $87,120 and her profits from $2,940 to $21,780. Today, she is a rich woman within her community.

All over the world, loans to women—which were formerly forbidden or could only be gotten with a husband's signature—

and loans to the poor are restructuring the third world economy.

Change the rules. Change the world. Seems to be working here.

11. Fractals & Chaos Mathematics. This paradigm shift is all about mathematics. The mathematics of fractals, a new kind of calculation that was made accessible by the ability of the computer to endlessly add numbers.

Fractal mathematics allows you to write a formula that when plotted on a computer screen will generate incredibly intricate patterns of extraordinary beauty. Using fractal math, you can also write a simple formula that will generate on the computer screen a picture of a fern or an oak tree or of clouds or of canyons as seen from thirty thousand feet. This is the mathematics of nature.

All around us are fractal patterns. What is a fractal? It is a simple pattern that if repeated enough times creates a highly complex and usually aesthetically pleasing image. Go look at an oak tree starting with the tiniest branch. You will note that the shape and structure of that branch is repeated in the next-larger branch and then in the next-larger branch and then in the whole tree. That is a fractal pattern.

Your circulatory system is fractal. Your heart beats in a fractal pattern. Water drips from a spigot fractally. It seems that everywhere we look, fractal patterns appear. And once you can use mathematics to deal with these patterns, you have a tremendous advantage for understanding and manipulation.

I predict that no industry, no business, no organization, will be unaffected by this new mathematics. This new way of describing the world mathematically has opened up whole new realms of problem solving. It is only in its fledgling state.

12. Personalized production. Take one hundred small advantages derived from the Total Quality movement; mix with a careful assessment of your customer. Add a visionary picture of the future and you get the new paradigm of production: a logical, rational, impossible paradigm: Build every product for just one person, the person who is buying it.   .

Ah, yes, utopia. But fantasy only? It is reality for the National Bicycle Industrial Company, a subsidiary of the electronics giant Matsushita. In a *Fortune* article, October 22, 1990, the process is described by Susan Moffat. The key is combining flexible manufacturing and CAD/CAM with highly skilled employees with modem links around the world.

The process starts with a person being "fitted" for the bike. Data on arm length, leg length, foot size, body weight, torso length, sex, and kind of bike needed are all sent to the factory via fax. There the facts are entered into a Digital Equipment Corporation minicomputer, which produces the blueprint and all necessary bar coding to track all the pieces.

From there the bike is assembled by top-quality craftspeople using the best automated equipment where appropriate and their own skills when needed. Total time for assembly: three hours. Cost to the customer—$545 to $3,200. A standard bike runs between $250 and $510.

Through this personal production method, the customer can choose between 11,231,862 variations of his or her bicycle.

Typical of the Japanese, once Matsushita gets the quirks worked out, they will move the concept to higher-profit products.

What more powerful way to deliver customer satisfaction than personal production. And coupled with Total Quality, it makes total sense for the twenty-first century.

13. "Masters and patrons." In the management field, I have seen a new paradigm that I believe will have enormous impact over the next ten years. Bill Weimer, whom I mentioned earlier in the book as a paradigm shifter within IBM, is now retired from IBM and sharing a concept of manager/employee relationship that offers fundamentally new rules for both.

He calls the relationship "masters and patrons." He draws on European history for his concept. By looking at how the master artists were enabled to do their great works, he discovered the coequal role of the patrons. Masters were enabled to do their best by patrons supporting them.

The masters of the modern age are the workers, the engineers, the scientists, the salespeople, the "doers" of the company or organization or culture. These masters, of course, would do things anyway, with or without patrons. But Weimer points out that a good patron optimizes the output of the masters.

Masters without patrons cannot do their best.

Patrons, on the other hand, without masters have nothing to do at all. Patrons protect the masters from people trying to take their time and resources. Patrons get the masters their resources from which they will construct their masterworks. Patrons protect the masters from the "trivial," which allows the masters to focus on the important.

Weimer's key point in this new paradigm is: Both are required to have optimized results.

For me, this is a brand-new (even though it is very old) way of looking at responsibilities in companies. Weimer levels the relationship between manager and worker. The new relationship clarifies roles in a positive light. It explicitly defines the work we have to do depending on our roles. And Weimer, who is full of insights on this topic, adds, it also reminds us that we can't be both master and patron at the same time.

What I like best about this new management paradigm is that everyone comes out more important.

14. Virtual reality. This last paradigm shift on my list is well known already. It is also perhaps the most dramatic, the most wide-ranging in its impact, the most significant in its potential to change the world. Its conceptual father is Jaron Lanier, founder of VPL Research, Inc., in Palo Alto, California.

Virtual reality uses three basic elements to create a world that doesn't exist. Let me explain. First you need a pair of "goggles" that fit over your eyes. The lenses of the goggles are actually TV screens, one for each eye. On top of the goggles is a motion-sensing device, so that if you turn your head or look up or down, the device registers that motion. The second element is a glove, the "dataglove," which has sensors built into it so that when you move your hand or point a finger or make a grip, the glove detects that motion. The third piece of the virtual reality equipment is a very fast image-calculating computer. In 1991 all this equipment costs about a quarter of a million dollars. By 1995, it will be below ten thousand dollars.

So what does all this equipment do? First the computer takes pictures from an inventory it has in storage and generates them on the two TV screens inside the goggles you are wearing. For instance, an architect may have been designing a new building. He has used the computer to create the blueprints and the perspective drawing for the building. The computer can take that data and imagery and manipulate it into many, many pictures from almost any angle, once it has the original image.

When you call up the initial image you want to look at, the computer creates two images (one for each screen in the goggles) and makes them just different enough so that for you it is stereoscopic—3D. When you turn your head, the computer senses that through the motion detector on the goggles, and it computes how those pictures should change to be consistent with how you turned your head. For you, it is as if you are looking out of the goggles through glass lenses at a world beyond you. You feel you are viewing something real, that is, "virtual reality."

Remember, the computer is generating the pictures. But it looks three-dimensional and it is so responsive that if you were to turn around in a complete circle, you would see 360 degrees of images. For all intents and purposes, you are now inside the computer. Science fiction writers have dubbed this "cyberspace."

What about the glove? That is how you touch and move things inside cyberspace. When you reach out, the glove senses your hand motion and, in your field of vision, a glove appears, computer-generated, of course. Point your finger at something you want to move toward, the computer senses the pointing and the direction and generates images that make you think you are moving toward the direction you have pointed. There are even ways of speeding up and slowing down. You can fly over the landscape, grab an object, turn it upside down.

And all the time the computer is updating the visual images fifteen to thirty times per second, almost as fast as in a movie. In Visual Reality, you can be in any world that can be imagined as long as the imaginer can put it into the computer in images that the computer can manipulate.

If it sounds like a game, it is, but so much more! Think about education: Put on your VRG (virtual reality gear) in chemistry and with your teacher by your "virtual" side, you can investigate the concept of atoms. Via special image-generating software in the computer, you can visit a water molecule. Look at the electron cloud. Examine the nucleus. Watch a chemical reaction between water and iron forming rust. Think about biology. No more vivisection. Instead with your virtual reality gear, you go inside a computer representation of the animal, see all the parts, watch the heart pump, watch the throat swallow, look out of the eye to see what the animal sees. Think about geography. Now you can go to see the Amazon, the barrens of Asia, the mountains of the moon. Think about mathematics; finally you will be able to see rendered in three dimensions what all those quadratic equations **look like**.

Think about the impact of virtual reality on training for businesses. For its impact on the movie industry. For sporting events. Think about its impact on designing new products. An architect takes the client for a walk through the building. A car designer takes the vehicle for a drive. The potential customer, too.

Think about the impact of virtual reality on the travel industry, both for better and for worse. I go via VRG instead of really going. I preview my trip with VRG to close the sale before I buy the tickets. It could work both ways.

Via virtual reality the entire communications/information industry will be fundamentally altered. Truly like nothing we've ever seen before.

And it is coming fast. All the necessary technology to make this paradigm shift low-cost and highly accessible is already trending down in price: small, high-resolution flat-screen TVs; fiber-optic sensors to embed in the glove; motion detectors based on solid-state chips; super-minicomputers on a chip—the Intel 586 or the next Motorola chip.

This is one I can't wait to see.

I could easily augment these fourteen with another thirty. I didn't mention such obvious and well-publicized paradigm shifts as nanotechnology, desktop prototyping, diamond-coating technologies, each of which is causing a revolution in industries around the world. But I am trying to make a point. It is your job to identify the paradigm shifts that will impact you. It's worth the work.

No matter how much you study the future, it will always surprise you; but you needn't be dumbfounded!—Kenneth Boulding

CHAPTER 14

And So It Goes

I WAS AT A LECTURE in 1975 when Dr. Boulding, a professor of economics, said that, and I thought how perfectly it explains why we spend time trying to discover the future. There will **always** be unanticipated events. That is the nature of the universe. But there are many events that can be anticipated if one takes the time to look for them. And the identification of those elements protects us from "dumbfoundedness." That is why the Paradigm Principles are so useful.

I have made the following points in this book about paradigms:

1. Our perceptions of the world are strongly influenced by paradigms.

2. Because we become so good at using our present paradigms, we resist changing them.

3. It is the outsider who usually creates the new paradigm.

4. Practitioners of the old paradigm who choose to change to the new paradigm early, must do so as an act of faith rather than as the result of factual proof, because there will never be enough proof to be convincing in the early stages.

5. Those who change to a successful new paradigm gain a new way of seeing the world and new approaches for solving problems as a result of the shift to the new rules.

6. A new paradigm puts everyone back to zero, so practitioners of the old paradigm, who may have had great advantage, lose much or all of their leverage.

As a conclusion to these observations, I have suggested that, in turbulent times, it is to your best advantage to develop and practice paradigm pliancy.

In *Ascent of Man,* Jacob Bronowski speaks to pliancy in his chapter, "Knowledge or Certainty." He focuses on the Heisenberg uncertainty principle and suggests it should be renamed the "principle of tolerance," which "fixed once and for all the realization that all knowledge is limited. It is the irony of history that at the very time when this was being worked out by physicists there should rise, under Hitler in Germany and other tyrants elsewhere, a counter-conception: a principle of monstrous certainty" (page 367).

The Hitlers of the world demonstrate both the worst kind of paradigm paralysis and what can happen when a person in power persuades others to join him in that belief. But the condition of despotic certainty can be found to a lesser degree in experts who choose to tell the rest of us why certain things are impossible.

To be tolerant to new ideas; to be tolerant of people who are suggesting those new ideas; to have tolerance toward people who see the world differently from your view: These are the key lessons of the Paradigm Principles.

Some people have mistakenly concluded from Kuhn's work and my comments on his work that "any" idea is right and that no idea is "righter" than any other. And some have even gone so far as to say that the deep significance of the Paradigm Principles is that there is no such thing as truth and falsity, right and wrong.

At the outer fringes, people like Werner Erhard, of *est* notoriety, have suggested that the true meaning of the Paradigm Principles is that we create the world we live in and that it is totally "subject" to our own mentality.

If there is one thing I am clear on it is: **We do not create the world around us. There is an objective, knowable universe.**

But the universe is highly complex and is not easily knowable. What we have been doing for our entire species' life is getting to know this huge and ancient reality of time and space. Slowly we accumulate wisdom about what it is. And as time passes and we study more and more, we will learn its secrets.

Fractal mathematics, which I cited as a paradigm shift in Chapter 13, is a perfect illustration of this growing body of knowledge. Who would have guessed that from a relatively simple set of iterations, an enormously complex picture would emerge. The key: time. And so we find that, within the mathematics of fractals, there is a way to grow complexity over time and create something as wonderful as the universe.

But there is so much left to know, to learn. And to have the openness to learn again, to resee what we've seen before in new light, to explore the new territories that open when we change our paradigms. That is our species' challenge and our quest. That is worth the time of the ages and generations upon generations of learning and effort.

I feel sorry for those who are certain that they know it all . . . now. At the very least, they will end up looking like fools; and at the worst, they block the serious examination of important but radical ideas.

In his book *Profiles of the Future*, Arthur C. Clarke builds two lists that exemplify this discussion. One list is of those inventions that had been expected during the twentieth century and the other is the list of discoveries or inventions no one ever mentioned:

The Expected	death rays
telephones	transmutation
automobiles	artificial life
flying machines	immortality
steam engines	invisibility
submarines	teleportation
robots	

The Unexpected
X rays
nuclear energy
radio
TV, electronics
quantum mechanics
relativity
transistors
masers and lasers
superconductors

atomic clocks
determining the composi-
tion of celestial bodies
neutrinos
dating the past with car-
bon 14
detecting invisible planets
the ionosphere
Van Allen belt
pulsars

Clarke composed these two lists in 1962, so there are other elements that could be added to the unexpected list that would make it even more dramatic. The point of the second list is simple: Perfect anticipation cannot be expected.

And, on top of that, one major unanticipated paradigm shift creates ripples of other changes that can make the future significantly different from an otherwise logical forecast without that major change incorporated. All the more reason for an open attitude.

An attitude of tolerance and openness keeps available the huge potential of conceptual leverage that springs from new ideas that can change the world, the very paradigm shifts that I have spent this book writing about.

Now it is time to acknowledge explicitly that which has been implicit in all that I have written. You probably have come to the conclusion that I have been offering for your consideration:

a paradigm of paradigms

I have been giving you a set of rules for understanding and manipulating paradigms. I have suggested the boundaries of this paradigm; I have suggested the problem-solving capability of this set of rules; I have offered anecdotes/models of how this paradigm works; and I have suggested to you that by using this conceptual framework you can dramatically improve your ability to explore the future.

What does this mean to you at this point? First, there is an act of faith that you will have to go through if you are going to use this paradigm. I have not given you enough proof to make you certain. And, second, only if you go out and try these rules for observing the world will you find out if I have given you something worthwhile. Only if you start solving problems that you couldn't solve before, explaining behaviors that you couldn't explain before, seeing the world in a new light and with new vision, will you become convinced of this paradigm's worth.

I have tried to offer you clear directives so you can become a better strategic explorer. I have based those directives on the Paradigm Principles.

The testing is up to you. I said at the outset that your single most important skill as a strategic explorer is to understand how your vision is shaped, what influences your perception. Without that understanding, all the other skills will be only minimally useful.

Let us reflect back on Peter Drucker's observation:

Significant competitive advantage lies with those organizations and individuals who anticipate well in turbulent times.

What I have been suggesting throughout this book is that much of the turbulence of our times is caused by: (1) the failures of old paradigms (and the attempts to prop up those outmoded rules), and (2) the creation and introduction of new paradigms.

While trends have made the headlines for the last couple of years, these are not the chief causes of turbulence. Trends are much easier to perceive because they have history, they leave a path from which we can forecast their direction.

> **Because trends have clear direction, instead of causing turbulence, they actually help reduce it because they have a significant amount of predictability.**

Even if we do not like the shape and content of the emerging trends, they at least give information that allows us to anticipate certain consequences. Of course, explosive trends can cause great turbulence; but most trends take time to gather momentum, and we can use that time to reduce their negative impacts on us and optimize the opportunities they hold for us.

Embedded in the paradigm discussion is a special kind of feedback loop for innovation, which James Bright, a pioneer in technology forecasting, has examined. One of Bright's observations about innovation is that it is spurred on by turbulence, or ''crisis,'' as he calls it.

In times of crisis (high turbulence), people expect, in fact demand, great change. This willingness to accept great change generates two results:

1. More people, responding to the demand for great change, put in time trying to find new ways, i.e., new paradigms, that will resolve the crisis, thus increasing the likelihood of paradigm shifts.

2. More people are willing, because of the crisis mentality, to accept fundamentally new approaches to solving the crisis, thus increasing the opportunity to change paradigms.

And this sets the stage for radical change. Let me give you the following sequence to think about:

Step 1 The established paradigm begins to be less effective.

Step 2 The affected community senses the situation, begins to lose trust in the old rules.

Step 3 Turbulence grows as trust is reduced (the sense of crisis increases in Bright's terms).

Step 4 Creators or identifiers of the new paradigm step forward to offer their solutions (many of these solutions may have been around for decades waiting for this chance).

Step 5 Turbulence increases even more as paradigm conflict becomes apparent.

Step 6 Affected community is extremely upset and demands clear solutions.

Step 7   One of the suggested new paradigms demonstrates ability to solve a small set of significant problems that the old paradigm could not.

Step 8   Some of the affected community accepts the new paradigm as an act of faith.

Step 9   With stronger support and funding, the new paradigm gains momentum.

Step 10   Turbulence begins to wane as the new paradigm starts solving the problems and the affected community has a new way to deal with the world that seems successful.

At this point, with the affected community increasingly comfortable with the new paradigm, the level of tolerance for more new ideas drops dramatically, and the cycle is complete. Now we must wait for the next round of significant problems that the newly accepted paradigm cannot solve to trigger a new cycle.

Obviously, during turbulent times, many more paradigms are going to be proposed than accepted.

Many are unsuccessful paradigms. Others are marginally acceptable. A few will become the prevailing paradigms. Our challenge as strategic explorers, whether our role is that of manager, politician, educator, or citizen, is to make it easier for the new paradigms to get a fair hearing and to help the paradigm shifters feel safer.

It is still a great risk in our society to offer new rules for the game.

One of my corporate clients responded to exactly this point and created a program that I think is exemplary. The specific division I was working with was known for its unwillingness to think radically, so the woman in charge of improving their attitude toward innovation created a Trial Balloon Day. On those days, about once per quarter, people could sign up and meet at an off-site location with an evaluation committee. The committee, schooled in the concept of paradigms and their influence, would listen to the new idea and examine its merits and risks with the innovator. If it was a good idea, the committee, plus the innovator, would carry it up two levels. If the idea was inappropriate, the innovator could leave anonymously—no embarrassment or funny stories and jokes behind his/her back. The response to the Trial Balloon Day has been very positive, because it reduces the risk of suggesting new paradigms.

It is this kind of willingness that we need throughout our society during these turbulent times. Because only if we are willing to look broadly at new ideas and new ways of solving problems, will we find the caliber of innovation that we will need to move successfully into the twenty-first century.

FINAL THOUGHTS

We live in a time of paradigm shifts. Not everyone can formulate successful new paradigms. Only a few do that. But all of us can be more open to looking for the changes, exploring them for their implications, and creating a supporting climate for the attempts. There is no question that, in many areas, we need new paradigms. In ever increasing frequency, the call for innovation goes out across the United States, and around the globe. Paradigm shifts are one of the key innovative behaviors.

Question: Who is scouting the future for us? Answer: Lots of people. What I mean is this: One person's paradigm shift may be another person's reality. Somewhere in the world, alternative paradigms are already part of a system. The United States is scouting the future of communications; France is scouting the future of debit cards; Japan has been scouting the future of participatory management; Argentina is scouting the future of inflation control; the Soviet Union is scouting the future of democracy. Just by looking around the world, we can find many other paradigms that may allow us to solve significant problems of our own.

Let me conclude this book by offering five quotes and one story.

"Speed is useful
only if you are running
in the right direction."—JAB

"It is important not to mistake
the edge of the rut
for the horizon."—ANONYMOUS

"Those who say it cannot be done
should get out of the way
of those who are doing it!"—ANONYMOUS

"The real act of discovery consists
not in finding new lands
but in seeing with new eyes."—MARCEL PROUST

"No corporation gets hit
by the future between the eyes,
they always get it in the temple!"—DICK DAVIS, consultant

This last quote is my favorite, because it's true for all of us, not just corporations. Looking forward only in one direction leads to a special kind of strategic blindness. One must scan the horizon constantly to identify the important changes occurring on the sidelines, at the edges. After all, isn't that what exploring is all about?

A FINAL STORY: THE PIG AND THE SOW

Once upon a time, there was a man who had a cabin in the mountains and a Porsche to get there. Every Saturday morning, he would drive up to his cabin on a very dangerous road filled with blind curves, unguarded drop-offs, and tricky turns.

But this man was not bothered by danger. After all, he had a great car to drive, he was an excellent driver, and he knew the road like the back of his hand.

One fine Saturday morning, he was driving to his cabin. He was coming up to one of his favorite blind curves. He slowed down, shifted gears, and put on the brakes in preparation for the turn that was about two hundred yards away. All of a sudden, from around that curve, came a car careening almost out of control! The car nearly went off the cliff but, at the last second, its driver pulled the car back onto the road. The car swerved into his lane, then back into its lane, then back into his lane again.

My God, he thought, I am going to be hit! So he slowed almost to a stop.

The car came roaring on toward him, swerving back and forth. Just before it was about to hit him—at the last moment—it swung back into its lane. As it went past him, a beautiful woman stuck her head out the window of the car and yelled at him at the top of her lungs, ''PIG!!''

What? he thought, How dare she call me that! He was incensed by her accusation! Instantly he yelled after her, ''SOW!!!'' as she continued down the road.

''I was in my lane! She was the one who was all over the place!'' he muttered to himself. Then he began to get control of his rage; he smiled and was pleased that at least she didn't get away without his stinging retort. He'd gotten her good, he thought smugly.

And with that, he put the accelerator to the floor, raced around that blind curve . . . **and ran into the pig**!

This is a paradigm story. He thought the woman was calling him a name. But she was really doing a heroic thing. In spite of the fact that she had almost been killed, she took the time to try to warn him about the pig on the road around the curve. But he had paradigm paralysis. He thought she called him a name; so he followed ''the rules'' and called her a name . . . and thought that was the end of it.

Actually, he had demonstrated the beginnings of some flexibility when he noticed that it was she, not he, who was swerving all over the road. If he had had paradigm pliancy, he would have responded to her shout by asking himself, **What is going on?** Then he would have driven around the corner much more cautiously. At the least, he would not have hit the pig. At the most, he could have stopped, picked the pig up, put it in his trunk, and driven away with it.

The moral: During the next decade many people will be coming around blind curves yelling things at you. They will be too busy to stop and explain, so it will be up to you to figure it out.

If you have paradigm paralysis, you will be hearing nothing but threats.

If you have paradigm pliancy, you will be hearing nothing but opportunity!

I would submit, in the context of all that I have said, that the choice of which you hear is entirely up to you.

Thank you for reading my book.

Afterword

IN THIS BOOK I have tried to indicate the power and influence of paradigms, to explain why we cling to our old paradigms, to suggest some reasons for being more open to new paradigms. I have stated that, during turbulent times, we need to actively search for and anticipate the future.

Now it is your turn to do some work. If you accept what I have been saying, then I would like you to do the following things:

Take an inventory of your present paradigms by writing down what you believe to be the "right" way of doing things or acting in the following areas:

- Your job especially the management style, (i.e., I believe in breaking deadlines rather than releasing shoddy products. When the product is excellent, and not before, is when it will be released)

- Your family life (i.e., close physical contact with my kids is a necessity for helping them grow up healthy)

- Your morals (i.e., lying always creates more problems than it solves)

- Your politics (i.e., a country without affordable legal protection for everyone cannot be a just country)

- Your religion (i.e., do unto others as you would have them do unto you)

- Your view of the rest of the world (i.e., most Asian cultures have a much stronger sense of the importance of a long-range vision of the future than Western culture. They are willing to think two hundred years ahead and plan for it)

Look for rules/beliefs that focus your attention and create the base by which you measure others. Any time you have a "Thou shalt not," you have part of a paradigm.

If you are married, you might ask your spouse to do the same thing. Comparing notes can be an insightful activity. By the way, one of the best tests of what your rules are is what you teach your children. You may break some of your own rules, but usually what you try to teach your children is what you hold others up to for judgment.

In addition to the above, there are two more exercises I would like you to do: Write a list of rules that other people practice but with which you disagree. This list will help identify areas of paradigm conflict for you.

Now ask yourself, what conditions would force you to alter your present paradigms? For instance, you may be against stealing, but, under certain conditions, you may find yourself willing to steal. This examination is very important because it allows you to explore conditions under which you would alter your present paradigms.

After you have listed the paradigms by which you direct your life, you can begin to monitor how they help you solve problems and how they get in the way of solving other problems. Once you are aware of your rules, you can look for changes in the world that may impact on your paradigms and challenge them. Or you can choose to start changing them for reasons of your own.

Remember what I said earlier: I am not against having paradigms; they help us deal much more effectively and efficiently with life. But I believe we need to keep flexing them and testing them in these turbulent times.

One more recommendation for those of you who want to do something with this concept: The cheapest, most powerful way to stretch your paradigms and improve your strategic exploration skills is to read. I read sixty publications per month (including four dailies), because it is my business to stay in touch with new ideas. I offer you a more modest goal. Below is a list of thirteen books to read and then nine publications to monitor (in order of priority).

BOOKS

Clarke, Arthur C. *Profiles of the Future*. Rev. ed. New York: Warner, 1985.
Drexler, K. Eric. *Engines of Creation*. New York: Anchor Press, 1986.

Drucker, Peter F. *Managing in Turbulent Times*. New York: Harper and Row, 1980.

Ferguson, Marilyn. *The Aquarian Conspiracy*. Los Angeles: Tarcher, 1980.

Garwood, David, and Michael Bane. *Shifting Paradigms: Reshaping the Future of Industry*. Stone Mountain, Ga.: Dogwood Press, 1990.

Harmon, Willis. *An Incomplete Guide to the Future*. New York: Norton, 1970.

Judson, H. F. *The Eighth Day of Creation*. New York: Simon and Schuster, 1979.

Kuhn, Thomas S. *The Structure of Scientific Revolutions*. Chicago: University of Chicago Press, 1970.

Langer, Ellen J. *Mindfulness*. Reading, Mass.: Addison-Wesley, 1989.

Meadow, Dennis, et al. *Limits to Growth*. New York: Signet, 1972.

Rheingold, Howard. *Virtual Reality*. New York: Summit Books, 1991.

Schumacher, E. F. *Small Is Beautiful*. New York: Harper and Row, 1972.

Toffler, Alvin. *The Third Wave*. New York: Morrow, 1980.

Each of these books presents a dramatic alternative to some of today's paradigms and will challenge many of your paradigms as they did mine. Check your response to their ideas. Find your boundaries. Consider theirs. You can't help but stretch.

PUBLICATIONS

The Christian Science Monitor, a daily, 1-800-456-2220. If I could choose only one publication to monitor future possibilities, this is it. Not only does it cover emerging technologies and social issues well, but it has a global perspective. No other publication even comes close to *CSM* in terms of its breadth and depth of exploration of important issues of the future.

Science News, a weekly, 1-800-247-2160. This little publication is usually only sixteen pages long, and summarizes brilliantly the new scientific and technological information of the past seven days. It is written for the lay person and has one major feature each time. The best bargain in science information.

The Atlantic Monthly, 1-800-525-0643. For technological types, this is your balancing publication. It regularly covers social/political issues of great future importance.

Mother Earth News, a bimonthly, P.O. Box 70, Hendersonville, NC 28739, 212-260-7210. Doing things differently is the mark of this publication. It is pro-environment, pro-small business, pro–self-reliance. It reflects the ideals and paradigms of a special minority in the United States and regularly describes important alternative ways to solve significant problems.

Popular Science, a monthly, Times Mirror Magazines, Inc., 380 Madison Avenue, New York, NY 10017. This publication has expanded its perspective in the past ten years and now reports not just "gee whiz" technology but a broad range of technologies. Its strength is that it is usually first to publish wild new inventions and innovations. It takes the time to illustrate and describe these concepts so that you can get a good idea of their possible applications.

The Wall Street Journal, a daily, 11 Cortlandt, New York, NY 10007. Too bad they don't publish a monthly summary of their great stories. Their Op-Ed page has great columns often suggesting major business paradigm shifts and, at least once a month, a front-page story gives insight into changes in the business world of which you should be aware.

The Futurist, a bimonthly, World Future Society Headquarters, 4916 St. Elmo Avenue, Bethesda, MD 20814-5089. This is the official publication of the World Future Society. While it could be stronger editorially, the concepts explored every other month are worth your time, if for no other reason than to see what the professionals are writing about. It regularly focuses on social/political innovations and their implications.

Technology Review, a bimonthly, 1-617-253-8292. While the above publications cover much of the emerging technological ideas, *Technology Review,* published by MIT, offers special insight because of the way it focuses with such depth on single issues. I have always found at least one important thought in every issue I've received.

New Sense Bulletin, a twice-monthly, Interface Press, 1-800-553-MIND; 213-223-2500. This nifty little four-page newsletter is the result of the efforts of the author of *The Aquarian Conspiracy,* Marilyn Ferguson. Beautifully summarized, the information is always at the edge of the brain-mind paradigm.

Bibliography

FOREWORD

Crosby, Philip B. *Quality is Free*. New York: McGraw Hill, 1979.

Deming, W. Edwards. *Out of the Crisis*. Cambridge, Mass: Massachusetts Institute of Technology: Center for Advanced Engineering Study, 1986.

Juran, Joseph M. *Juran on Planning for Quality*. New York: Free Press, 1988.

CHAPTER 1

Galling, Walter, and Robert Ball. "How Omega and Tiscot Got Ticking Again." *Fortune*, January 14, 1980, pp. 68–70.

CHAPTER 2

Drucker, Peter. *Managing in Turbulent Times*. New York: Harper & Row, 1980.

Toffler, Alvin. *Future Shock*. New York: Random House, 1970.

CHAPTER 3

Ferguson, Marilyn. *The Aquarian Conspiracy*. Los Angeles: J. P. Tarcher, 1980.

Harmon, Willis. *An Incomplete Guide to the Future*. New York: W. W. Norton, 1970.

Kuhn, Thomas S. *The Structure of Scientific Revolutions*. Chicago: University of Chicago Press, 1970.

Naisbitt, John. *Megatrends: Ten New Directions Transforming Our Lives*. New York: Warner Books, 1982.

Smith, Adam. *Power of the Mind*. New York: Ballantine Books, 1975.

CHAPTER 4

Kuhn, Thomas S. *The Structure of Scientific Revolutions*. Chicago: University of Chicago Press, 1970.

CHAPTER 5

Kuhn, Thomas S. *The Structure of Scientific Revolutions*. Chicago: University of Chicago Press, 1970.

Strowger, Almon B. Strowger was a mortician in Kansas City and patent holder of the switching system used by Bell Telephone in the late nineteenth century. Received his patent in 1889. See *A History of Technology. Vol. VII: The Twentieth Century*. Clarendon Press, 1978, p. 1245.

CHAPTER 6

Imai, Masaaki. *Kaisen: The Key to Japan's Competitive Success*. New York: McGraw-Hill, 1986.

Kuhn, Thomas S. *The Structure of Scientific Revolutions.* Chicago: University of Chicago Press, 1970.

CHAPTER 7

Cerf, Christopher, and Victor Navasky. *The Experts Speak.* New York: Pantheon Books/Random House, 1984.

Kuhn, Thomas S. *The Structure of Scientific Revolutions.* Chicago: University of Chicago Press, 1970.

CHAPTER 8

Ansberry, Clare. "Steel Industry Is on the Verge of David vs. Goliath Test: Tiny NUCOR Corp. Has Forged Revolutionary Route to Future." *The Wall Street Journal,* October 17, 1989 (CCXIV:75), p. A5.

Browning, E. S. "Japanese Triumph: Sony's Perseverance Helped to Win Market for Mini-Compact Disk Players; Firm Worked for Years on N. V. Philips Invention: U.S. Firms Quit Trying: One Hurdle: Think Small." *The Wall Street Journal,* February 27, 1986 (CCVII: 40), p. 1.

Chase, William G., and Herbert, Simon. "Perception in Chess." *Cognitive Psychology,* January 1973 (Vol. 4), pp. 55–81.

Fisher, Arthur. "Science News—New Airbag Concept." *Popular Science,* July 1984, p. 10.

Keebler, Jack. "Low-Cost, Low-Tech Airbag." *Popular Science,* September 1985, p. 30.

Kuhn, Thomas, S. *The Structure of Scientific Revolutions.* Chicago: University of Chicago Press, 1970.

Langer, Ellen. *Mindfulness.* Reading, Mass.: Addison Wesley, 1989.

McCready, Paul. "Human Nature: The Floating Needle." *Science Digest,* March 1983, pp. 10, 52.

Medvedev, G. "Chernobyl Notebook." *Soviet Union Economic Affairs,* June 1989, pp. 1–75.

Schaef, Ann Wilson. *Women's Reality: An Emerging Female System in a White Male Society.* New York: Harper & Row, 1985.

Twain, Mark. *Life on the Mississippi.* New York: Oxford University Press, 1990.

CHAPTER 9

Garwood, David, and Michael, Bane. *Shifting Paradigms: Reshaping the Future of Industry.* Greensboro, N.C.: Dogwood Press, 1990.

Pirsig, Robert. *Zen and the Art of Motorcycle Maintenance.* New York: William Morrow, 1974.

Rand, Ayn. *Atlas Shrugged.* New York: Random House, 1957.

Taylor, Frederick W. *The Principles of Scientific Management.* New York: Harper & Row, 1911.

CHAPTER 10

Johnson, J. T. "The Hot Path to Solar Electricity." *Popular Science,* May 1990, pp. 82–85.

CHAPTER 11

Bronowski, Jacob. *Ascent of Man.* Boston: Little, Brown, 1973.

Clarke, Arthur C. *Profiles of the Future.* New York: Holt, Rinehart, and Winston, 1984.

Horgan, John. "Profile: The Reluctant Revolutionary." *Scientific American,* May 1991, pp. 40–41.

CHAPTER 12

Bennis, Warren. "Leadership in the 21st Century." *Training,* May 1990, pp. 231–234.

CHAPTER 13

The Realization of World Economics

Cody, Edward. "The Future Isn't What It Used to Be." *The Washington Post National Weekly Edition,* February 5–11, 1990, p. 8.
Ohmae, Kenichi. "Toward a Global Regionalism." *The Wall Street Journal,* April 27, 1990, Op. Ed. page.

1. Solar Hydrogen Fission

Booth, William. "The Greenhouse Effect Is Making Nuclear Power Look Good." *The Washington Post National Weekly Edition,* August 28–September 3, 1989, p. 38.
Hansen, Kent et al. "MIT Report, Making Nuclear Power Work: Lessons from Around the World." *Technology Review,* February/March 1989, p. 29.
Lipkin, Richard. "A Safer Breed of Reactor in Sight." *Insight,* January 23, 1989, p. 52.

Pendleton, Scott. "Nuclear Enters a New Era." *The Christian Science Monitor,* March 6, 1991, p. 12.

Spinrad, Bernard I. "U.S. Nuclear Power in the Next Twenty Years." *Science,* February 12, 1988 (Vol. 239), p. 707.

Winslow, Ron. "New Breeder Reactor May Operate More Safely, Produce Less Waste." *The Wall Street Journal,* December 1, 1988, p. B4.

2. Time Taxes

Littleton, Colorado experiment in school system. Contact person Karla Langton, Office of Community Relations, Littleton School Board; 303-795-7007 x461.

3. Buffalo Commons

Bovard, James. "Put Agriculture Policy Out to Pasture." *The Wall Street Journal,* February 4, 1988, Op Ed page.

Eisenberg, Evan. "Back to Eden." *Atlantic,* November 1989, pp. 57–89. Wes Jackson's Land Institute is in Salinas, Kansas.

Knickerbocker, Brad. "A Century After the West Was Won." *The Christian Science Monitor.* December 18, 1990, pp. 11–12.

Tonge, Peter. "Making Good Impressions." *The Christian Science Monitor,* November 4, 1986, p. 23.

5. Magical Mystery Polymers

Amato, Ivan. "Materials Science—Designing Polymers for Structural Jobs." *Science,* November 24, 1990, p. 333.

Cherfas, Jeremy. "Stretching the Point." *Science,* February 9, 1990 (Vol. 247), p. 630.

Flam, Faye. "Plastics Get Oriented—and Get New Properties."
    Science, February 22, 1991 (Vol. 251), p. 874.
Hamilton, David P. "Toward the Polymer Chip." *Science,* Sep-
    tember 14, 1990, p. 1249.
"Notes—Plastic Bridges." *Technology Review,* October 1990,
    p. 80.
"Science and Technology: The Right Stuff, Composite Materials
    Will Make It One Day." *The Economist,* November 24,
    1990, p. 95.

6. Nature's Wisdom

Abelson, Philip H. "Medicine from Plants." *Science,* February
    2, 1990 (Vol. 247, No. 4942), p. 513.
Chen, Ingfei. "Plants Bite Back." *Science News,* December 22
    and 29, 1990 (Vol. 138) p. 408.
Cowen, Ron. "Medicine on the Wild Side: Animals May Rely
    on Natural Pharmacy." *Science News,* November 3, 1990
    (Vol. 138), p. 280.
Golden, Frederic. "Clever Kanzi." *Discover,* March 1991,
    p. 20.
Hall, Alan, ed. "Picking Insecticides Right Off the Tree." *Sci-
    ence and Technology,* November 4, 1985, p. 107.

7. Negawatts

Lovins, Amory. "Negawatts." *Across the Board,* September
    1990, p. 22. Published by the Conference Board, 845 Third
    Avenue, New York, NY 10022-6601; 212-759-0900.

8. New Building Materials

Free, John. "Dirt Cheap." *Popular Science,* November 1986,
    p. 16D.

Lampe, David. "Grow Your Own Buildings." *The Mother Earth News,* March/April 1980, p. 118.

9. Gaia

Kasting, James F. "Earth, the Living Planet: How Life Regulates the Atmosphere." *Planetary Report,* January/February 1990 (Vol. 10, No. 1), p. 8.

Lovelock, James E. *The Ages of Gaia, A Biography of Our Living Planet.* New York: Bantam, 1990.

10. Loans to Third World

Germani, Clara. "Poor Take Micro-Steps Off Welfare." *The Christian Science Monitor,* July 30, 1991, p. 12.

Massing, Michael. "Structural Adjustment in the Third World Has Been a Bust." *The Washington Post National Weekly Edition,* December 31, 1990–January 6, 1991, p. 24.

Pandya, Meenal. "Giving Women Access to Credit." *World Monitor*, March 1991, p. 18.

Press, Robert M. "Kenyans Thrive on Loan Program." *The Christian Science Monitor,* April 4, 1991, p. 9.

Stetson, Marnie. "Giving Credit Where It's Due." *World Watch,* March/April 1991, p. 7.

11. Fractals and Chaos

Folger, Tim. "Beyond Chaos." *Discover*, January 1991, p. 68.

Gleick, James. *Chaos, Making a New Science.* New York: Viking Penguin, 1987.

Maddox, John. "Order in the Midst of Chaos." *Nature*, October 4, 1990 (Vol. 347), p. 421.

Peterson, Ivars. "Ribbon of Chaos." *Science News*, January 26, 1991 (Vol. 139), p. 60.

12. Personalized Production

Moffat, Susan. "Japan's New Personalized Production." *Fortune*, October 22, 1990, p. 132.

13. Masters and Patrons

Weimer, William. *Masters and Patrons*. Atlanta: Dogwood Press, in press.

14. Virtual Reality

Daviss, Bennett. "Illusions—Reality Isn't Always What You Want It to Be. But Artificial Reality Is. Welcome to the Future." *Discover,* June 1990, p. 37.

Peterson, Ivers. "Recipes for Artificial Realities." *Science News,* November 24, 1990 (Vol. 138), p. 328.

Rheingold, Howard. *Virtual Reality*. New York: Summit Books, 1991.

"Science and Technology: The Unreal Thing." *The Economist*, September 15, 1990, p. 107.

Stix, Gary. "Reach Out—Touch Is Added to Virtual Reality Simulations." *Scientific American,* February 1991, p. 134.

Tisdale, Sallie. "It's Been Real—Real What Is the Question: How a Promising Twenty-First-Century Technology Is Being Devoted to an Expensive Toy for Technoweenies Called Virtual Reality." *Esquire,* April 1991, p. 32.

CHAPTER 14

Bronowski, Jacob. *Ascent of Man*. Boston: Little, Brown, 1973.

Clarke, Arthur C. *Profiles of the Future*. New York: Holt, Rinehart and Winston, 1984.

Drucker, Peter F. *Managing in Turbulent Times*. Harper & Row, 1980.

Index

"If you do plan to spend the rest of your life in the future, Joel Barker can show you how to understand and manage its potential more easily, more progressively, and more profitably."

—TOM BROWN, PH.D.
Management consultant, educator, and writer

"Joel's book was thought provoking; it provided a new way of looking at things for me and my managers."

—DUANE HARTLEY
Laboratory Director
Hewlett-Packard

"The key point to me is that the understanding of paradigms is crucial in helping people listen (openly) to new ideas . . . quality, leadership, organizational change, communication skills, and so on. So, it's a must-read!"

—DON SCOTT
Captain, U.S. Navy (Ret.)
Bay Area Quality Council

"A very powerful insight into change . . . It has significantly influenced my thinking and work in strategic planning for almost a decade."

—L. H. SIEVE
Director of Planning,
Consumer Foods Technology and Operations
General Mills, Inc.